The A-Z
OF
MINISTRY
WITH
CHILDREN

Winford Church

The A-Z OF MINISTRY WITH CHILDREN

Owen Shelley

Scripture
Union

Scripture Union books are published by
ANZEA PUBLISHERS
3-5 Richmond Road
Homebush West   NSW   2140
Australia

ISBN 0-85892-469-2

Cover design and illustration by Stephen Stanley
Illustration on page 172 by Dorothy Lewis
Typeset by Egan-Reid Limited, Auckland, New Zealand
Printed in Australia by Southwood Press Pty Limited, Marrickville, NSW.

CONTENTS

ACKNOWLEDGMENTS

My thanks go to John Lane and Karen Trutwein for extensive editing; to Keith Thompson for the illustrations in 'Finding a new angle', 'Lost and found', 'Propitiation', 'Quick sketching' and 'Redeemer'; to Joan Llewellyn and Virginia Coy for typing and correction; and to all those who have been my fellow labourers in the ranks of the CSSM and Scripture Union over the many years that I have been privileged to be a staff member of the movement.

MEMORIES

'When are you going to write your memoirs?' asked Allan Wallace, one of my old Toowoon Bay beach mission team members. 'Never!' I replied. 'No-one would want to read them.'

'I'd read them!' said Allan.

John Lane, who edited the material for *A to Z*, encouraged me to add something of my own experience, hence the inclusion of the introductory autobiographical notes. Remembering Allan's remark I am assured of at least one reader.

Beach missions

'I have much pleasure in announcing that, as from today, Owen is a member of the staff of the CSSM.' With these words my life as a full-time children's missioner began. It was New Years' Day 1954 at Palm Beach, north of Sydney. Basil Williams, the General Secretary of the Scripture Union and CSSM, told the news to the members of the beach mission team I was leading. That was my third stint as leader, following initial beach mission involvement at Austinmer in the summer of 1950/1951.

At the time that I joined the staff, Scripture Union ran eleven missions on the coast stretching from Harrington in the north to Huskisson in the south. During my first year, while on a visit to schools on the far north coast, I was asked 'Why doesn't the CSSM hold a mission at Evan's Head? It's the largest camping area on the coast!'

A little over twelve months later Evan's Head mission was launched. It is difficult now to understand the logistics of establishing a new work that was almost five hundred kilometres beyond our furthest outpost. Much of the Pacific Highway was still a gravel road in those days it took the best part of two tedious days to reach our destination.

Our team of fifteen men and eight women felt very much like David facing Goliath when we finally arrived at the camping area. At that time it held a thousand tents and caravans and we felt overwhelmed by its sheer size. On arrival we were greeted by Arthur Felsch who with a group of local farmers had spent all day chopping down lantana to clear enough space for us to erect our tents. We were in fact near the camping area but not a part of it.

Arthur said that the previous year on Boxing Day he had been picnicking at Evans Head with his family. Bored with sitting around he prayed, 'Lord, please give me something useful to do for you on Boxing Day.' The Lord answered his prayer in no uncertain manner. Arthur became the key person in the spread of missions on the far north coast, helping to develop not only Evans Head, but Brunswick Heads, Byron Bay, Ballina and Lennox Head as well.

Evans Head mission, in its first year, recorded the highest attendance of any beach mission with crowds of eight hundred to a thousand people gathering on the beach each day. With decorated beach pulpits, sand text competitions, puppets and quick sketching, much of our presentation was entirely new to the people who came along. Indeed some were even suspicious that we might be 'commos'!

We had our share of technical hitches. I recall making frantic efforts to hold the attention of a crowd of over a thousand who had gathered for our film night while Mr Singh, a local businessman, struggled to solve a problem with his projector. I finally had to apologise and dismiss the crowd.

The following year he told me, 'I've brought two projectors with me this time to be on the safe side!'

Famous last words! When the time came neither projector would operate. The local power supply may have had something to do with the problem.

Over the years I have never stayed longer than four years at a beach mission site; I am better at pioneering a work, then passing on the leadership to someone else. A group of us from Evans Head moved on to establish a new work at Sawtell and after only one summer at that site some of us moved again to start another mission at South West Rocks. In the development of beach missions in NSW this team was a highly significant one, due mainly to the presence of Peter Anderson (now a surgeon in Tamworth).

Peter was full of ideas and he developed techniques for rounding up a crowd to attend a meeting (known now in beach mission circles as 'scooping'). When after 3 years Peter took over the leadership from me, he boosted the daily attendance at 'Keenites' from a gratifying 150 to 250 in his first year. While we had been very thorough in 'scooping' the camping area, he hired a bus and gathered children from the township of South West Rocks as well. This is a good example of what can be achieved with vision coupled with enthusiasm—two very important qualities for children's workers.

Peter also introduced a separate tent for teenagers to meet in. He installed an ice-chest for drinks and an old record player and erected a sign which read —

Brubeck for free,
Coke for cash,
Come and see
Or else gate crash.

The experiment proved extremely successful in attracting teenagers and 'Teen Tents' became a standard fixture of most beach missions.

The following summer I visited each of the missions from Nambucca Heads to the Queensland border. The beach missions executive committee had suggested that I should be one of those who trialled my proposed scheme of Regional Advisers.

I didn't relish the role of official visitor, but it had its lighter side. At Byron Bay I drew the attention of the leader Rowland Croucher to the messy appearance of their marquee.

'I've asked the folk to collect their things but it doesn't seem to have much effect,' he replied.

'What I would do is collect all the personal property that is lying around and auction it back to them for three pence an item!'

'Good idea!' said Rowly. 'I'll try it'.

At breakfast the following morning the auction began.

'Whose are these?' asked Rowly, holding up a pair of shoes. No-one spoke. 'Surely they belong to somebody!'

It was then that the light dawned.

'Oh! They're mine!' I exclaimed.

This admission was greeted with hilarity and the team insisted that I should be charged three pence for each shoe.

My next target for beach mission expansion was the Port Stephens area. Over the next four years we saw the development

of four new centres: Shoal Bay, Halifax Park, Fingal Bay and Soldiers Point.

At Shoal Bay Harold Borig was equipment officer. Much of the equipment belonged to Harold, and to ensure its safety he marked each item with his name. At mealtimes the team had great fun calling out 'Would you pass the Borig please' when requesting the salt, pepper, sugar and so on. The equipment officers are the unsung heroes of beach mission, many of them, like Harold, serving behind the scenes for years.

Often the people who profit most from beach mission are the team members themselves. Many develop skills of communication that might otherwise remain dormant all their lives. One of the team at Shoal Bay who was rostered to give a talk at a beach service came to me about a hour beforehand.

'I can't do it!' he exclaimed.

No matter how I tried to persuade him he couldn't face it, and I had to step in at the last moment and give the talk myself. Despite this setback we continued to encourage him, working him in little by little to up-front responsibilities until he was able to overcome his nervousness. A couple of years later it was very satisfying to hear a new team member comment, 'I wish I could talk to kids like David can!'

For many team members, beach mission not only helps develop communication skills, but proves to be a time of deepening spiritual commitment and growth. David Claydon, who was State Director of Scripture Union NSW for a number of years, later became Federal Secretary of the Church Missionary Society. This role brought him into contact with missionaries serving in many parts of the world. He told me at the time that he had known many of them as members of beach mission teams in previous years.

I cannot let the subject of beach missions pass without some reference to tents. Tents of varying sizes are a focal point of beach mission activity and tent stories are legion. My first experience of erecting a big marquee was at Palm Beach. We laid out the canvas, banged in the pegs, attached the ropes and erected the walls.

'Where are the centre poles?' I asked.

Everyone looked puzzled until someone remembered that they had been carried under the tray of the truck that had delivered our gear. Obviously they were still there and had gone back to the city with the truck.

'I've got a mate with a utility' said one of the team. 'I'll ring him and get him to collect them for us.'

The sequel to the story was that the 'mate' was unable to find the caretaker at Chambers trucking yard and had to break in to the truck shed. He found our poles and in due course delivered them to us.

To my mind well erected tents reveal that we are competent campers who know what we are about. This is an important part of our witness in the camping area. Knowing my standards, one of my team organised the erection of a tent with infinite care. When they had finished, he called me over to display their handiwork.

'John, that's terrific! I've never seen a tent erected so neatly.'

John began to smile with pleasure.

'But you're going to have to pull it down again!'

His face fell.

'Why, what's the matter?' he asked.

'You've put it up inside out!' I replied.

I have always insisted that teams should let the children help with things like tent erection. It gives them the feeling of belonging. Once at Shoal Bay I erected six small marquees by myself with the help of a crowd of camping area children.

Children love to be noticed, children love to be useful, children love to be involved. Never say 'Out of the way, you kids.' Find something they can do and they will reward you with their loyal support. The loyalty of children is something to count on, as the following story shows.

We arrived at Toowoon Bay one year to discover that the

camping area had changed hands. The new proprietor had planned some events for the residents of the camp that clashed with our proposed program. Some team members had long faces.

'What are we going to do? He has roller skate races planned for the same time as our lantern procession.'

'What are you worried about?' I exclaimed. 'These are our kids! They come every year! We can bank on their loyalty.'

The outcome was that I offered the services of our team to help organise the races. Big Daryl, one of our group, was a keen skater, so we paraded through the area challenging all comers to race him. At race time the starting line was packed with competitors.

With the help of the team I took charge of marshalling the skaters while the caretaker and some of the parents supervised the judging at the other end of the course. I pushed the events through at a goodly pace, and finally when darkness fell I announced, 'Righto everybody! That's the last race. We're going to hold the lantern procession now! Everybody down to the big marquee!'

Moments later the race track was deserted.

One of the strengths of beach mission work is the team's identity with the rest of the campers. On the day of our arrival at Hawk's Nest my son Robert, then only two years of age, wandered away. While I was searching for him around the area one of the team caught up with me to say that he had been found. Returning to our quarters I found Robert safe and sound in the company of another toddler of about his own age. I then had to call at the tents to enquire whether anybody was missing a small boy until his family was finally found.

The result of this event was a considerable degree of warm hearted acceptance on the part of the people of the area and not a few chuckles. This made our task of knocking on tent doors to introduce ourselves very easy that year.

One of the most impressive features of beach mission work is its consistency, with teams returning to the same centre year after year. It was a very special pleasure to be invited to share in the celebration of Toowoon Bay's fortieth consecutive year of operation.

Phil Lamb, the leader, arranged with a local circus to 'borrow' an elephant. This was scooping at its best, as the campers turned out in full force to witness the event. What a privilege to stand on the park's climbing equipment and tell that huge crowd of the love of God in sending his Son to redeem us.

The camping areas along our coastline are one of the few frontiers where church people come into direct contact with those who have no commitment to the Christian faith.

Terry and Rob were two boys who responded to our teaching at Palm Beach mission. In the ensuing months they witnessed to their parents about their new found faith. Later that year their mother was hospitalised under the care of a Christian doctor who led her to the Lord. In telling me her story she described the joy that she now shared with her sons.

'The boys and I are praying for Dad' she said.

Camps

My first contact with the Scripture Union movement came through a friend, Ron ('Searg') Hayman, who invited me to join the team of a boys camp at The 'Grange', Mt Victoria. My first reaction was to say, 'What, spend a week playing games with a crowd of little kids!'

He persisted and I found that camps were entirely different from what I had imagined. I was hooked.

That first camp was led by a policeman named Athol Gordon whose hobby was taking 8mm movies. On one of our hikes through the bush we came to a fine stand of eucalyptus saplings and I challenged the boys to a climbing race. In those days I could shin up trees like a monkey, so I had no difficulty in demonstrating my climbing superiority. My triumph was short lived, however, as an excited group of boys attempted to shake me out of the tree. I clung to the branches for dear life until Athol called for restraint and I was able to slide down to safety. All of this was duly recorded on film and, whenever it was shown, Athol enjoyed hitting the reverse switch so that at the point of sliding down I was seen to shoot up the tree again at astonishing speed. So much for my film career!

Program planning and team meetings were unheard of in those days and I remember that on our arrival at about my third camp as an officer at camp, Athol announced, 'Righto Adjy, get the camp going!'

We team members looked at one another wondering who it was that he was addressing, until he indicated that I had been appointed adjutant i.e. second in command, and was expected to run things. I was to serve with a number of other leaders before finally being appointed as the Commandant of Saratoga junior boys camp on the shores of Brisbane Waters. At least I served a longer apprenticeship in camps than had been the case with beach missions.

In the providence of God, Norman Skinner joined the team that year. He was everything that I was not: organised, methodical and able to anticipate what was needed to ensure the smooth running of the camp. He became my partner for the first thirteen camps that I directed.

While Saratoga was a delightful location, the camp site itself was most unsuitable accommodation for a large group by modern day standards. A single bathroom with no shower was the only washing facility. Bath night was a real circus. The water had to be heated in the copper in the laundry and carried in by bucket to fill the bath. We organised the boys, fortunately only juniors, to bathe three at a time. Some of the team kept replenishing the water supply, others of us lathered heads ensuring that the boys were well scrubbed, while others supervised the towelling down.

'Right, you're out! Next one!' I roared. It was absolutely chaotic but great fun. My wife's recollections aren't as rosy. She was cook for the camp and because there was no refrigerator the meat went off! Phew!

Looking back on my early life I realise that much of the experience gained in my youth was ideal preparation for the task to which God had called me, especially on the camping side. My ambition from childhood, to be a farmer, led me to study firstly at Hurlstone Agricultural High School and then at Hawkesbury Agricultural College. On graduation I turned my hand to a variety of agricultural jobs.

This background earned me ready acceptance among country people when I began to travel throughout the bush conducting missions. One such instance was when I went to the little township of Yeoval to preach at the Sunday morning service. Afterwards I joined a group of the men who were standing outside chatting.

'Been out this way before?' one of them asked, a question that is very commonly on the lips of country people.

'Well, no, I've never been to Yeoval but I put in a couple of seasons on the harvest up Gollan way.' I replied.

'You've had to go at the wheat!' exclaimed another. The group recognised that I understood their world and I sensed their immediate acceptance.

My knowledge of things agricultural led me to organise the first of the agricultural camps that Scripture Union has conducted throughout NSW. A delegate at a conference I attended described how they had structured their camp program into interest clubs.

'One of the most successful ones was a farmer's club,' he explained.

I pondered, if a farmer's club was so successful why not structure the whole of a camp activity around a farming theme? A discussion of the idea with the boys of the ISCF at Hurlstone Agricultural High School led to the planning of the first agricultural camp, held at Richmond with twenty boys and six officers.

One officer was Milton Walker, later the driving force behind the development of agricultural camps until his tragic death in the Granville train disaster.

Two years later we had seventy applicants for a camp that could only take thirty. Perhaps this overwhelming response was due to the wording of the camp brochure, which read:

> Go north young man
> Go north to Goonoo Goonoo.

In subsequent years the agricultural camps under Tony's direction developed the concept of 'cluster' camping, successfully copied by other Scripture Union camps. The Agricultural Camp also pioneered the idea of a 'specialist' camp focusing on one major activity. Later came others like Arts Camp and Camp Technology. The leaders were selected for their ability in their field of interest and at camp they used their professional skills to the full.

As well as the agricultural camps, I continued to run a junior boys camp in September at the Grange in the Blue Mountains. In the summer I rounded up a large contingent to camp at Camp Bevington. Imagine my dismay when I arrived at the camp-site and discovered that a bushfire had raced through, destroying everything except the cook house and store shed. At the site we were greeted by a blackened group—Ron Hayman and some boys from Trinity Grammar School who had come up the previous day to erect the tents. They had spent their time cutting new tent poles and we had to resurrect the site from the ashes before we could begin our program. It was late that night before any of us headed for bed.

The following year I started the Pioneer Canoe Camp on the Shoalhaven River near Nowra.

The brochure trumpeted, 'We've found it—the camp-site of your dreams' and went on to extol the beauties of the meandering river. Our first camp was packed and in following years it always posted the 'full house' sign.

For me the most memorable year at Pioneer Canoe Camp was the summer of '62. Due to the drenching rain our peaceful river rose twenty feet overnight and became a raging torrent. I was away from the camp on a bivouac trip when the worst of the deluge hit. On our return I was greeted by my adjutant, Geoff Grimes, who had been left in charge.

'We've got problems!' he announced.

'You've got problems! What do you mean? Look at us! There's not one of us with a dry item of clothing or sleeping gear, everything is saturated!' I exclaimed.

'Well, our problem is that the cook is threatening to go home! I've been able to persuade him to stay till you got back but then he's off,' Geoff replied.

A camp without a cook did present a real problem.

'Leave him to me,' I muttered.

After a hasty consultation with 'Searg', I headed for the cook house, wearing nothing but a pair of underpants, a hat, and boots with no socks. As I entered the cook house I threw back my raincape exposing my manly torso. The water dripped off my cape and hat and flowed out of my boots.

'Boy! Cookie! Are we glad to see you! We haven't had a decent meal in two days. . .'

I laid it on thick and fast and Cookie couldn't get a word in edgewise. I was just running out of things to say when Ron appeared at the kitchen window. Though a little more respectably attired than I was, he still looked like the proverbial drowned rat.

'Wow! Cookie! Are we glad to see you!'

He launched into his pre-arranged spiel. Before he had finished, the cook was busily dicing vegetables.

'Do you think the boys would like a big pot of stew?' he asked. There wasn't a word about his resignation. I guess everybody likes to be appreciated!

My preference in camping is the smaller more intimate bushwalking group, rather than the larger more organised camp that, of necessity, runs to a time-table with whistles, bells, orderly duties and official 'lights out'. Frequently it is adversity (mostly rain) that brings the group together and creates a feeling of camaraderie. Years later when I meet and reminisce with some of the campers who shared these adventures, there is an immediate rapport.

One such memorable incident occurred on the 'Jungle Safari' in the MacPherson Ranges on the Queensland border. Deluging rain turned the jungle into a squelchy quagmire and after three days of growing web feet we were delighted to make it back to open country. We pitched our tents in a paddock on a deserted farm and settled down for the night.

In the early hours of the morning I was woken by the eerie sound of dingoes howling. Later when my companions began to stir, I asked 'Did anyone hear the dingoes last night?'

'Did I what?' exclaimed Ron. 'I've never heard anything more terrifying!' A short time later Ron strolled down to one of the other tents which was occupied by a group of boys, all local to the area.

'Anyone hear the dingoes last night?' asked Ron.

'What dingoes?' said one of the boys.

'A whole pack of them!' replied Ron. 'I was wondering where I'd left the machete so I'd have something to protect myself with!'

'Aw, they're nothing!' retorted one of the group. 'They howl around our farm all night every time there's a full moon!'

My nickname among bushwalking friends was 'Chief Big Rain on the Tail' as bad weather always seemed to be our lot. One year I planned a Warrumbungles Walkabout. We arranged to meet at Strathfield railway station and on arrival I was greeted by catcalls from the campers.

'Here he is!' they jeered. 'Looks like we'll be in for a wet camp!'

I assured the boys that the west was in the grip of a severe drought and that for once there was little likelihood of rain. You've guessed it! It turned out to be a wet week!

Despite the rain we had a super time and I remember vividly our final morning. I left the group early to go back to the car park and retrieve a vehicle so that we could run a shuttle service back to our cars. I drove around to the camping area where I had arranged to meet our party and waited for them to appear. Soon the sound of singing echoed down the valley. People staying at the camping ground peeked from their tent doors to see what was going on, as down the track our campers tramped, filling the bush with the melodious sound of 'Woad' and other camping songs. I had a lump in my throat as I watched them. What an inestimable privilege it has been to spend my life for and with groups of lads like these.

One of my regular campers said to me once 'You have a wonderful life! A lifetime of holidays!' Mind you I don't recall every incident with nostalgia. Camp leaders, especially directors are often the target of pranks. Most of the time I've been one jump ahead, but I was caught badly once. Our group was sleeping on the floor of the Lion's Club hall in Bellingen and when bedtime came the boys, for once, were already bunked down. That alone should have made me suspicious. As I slid into my sleeping bag the soles of my feet were tickled by stinging nettles. I froze and asked as casually as possible, 'Who is going to put out the lights?'

Before anyone could reply I said, 'It's OK, I'll do it!'

I wriggled out of my bag and switched out the lights, then padded into the kitchen, walking as normally as possible despite the agonising pain in my feet. I turned on taps, rattled pots and pretended to be busy. Finally, when I sensed that everyone was asleep, I crept out and removed the nettles with the satisfaction of having prevented the boys from knowing I'd been caught in their trap.

Controversies

In the early 1960's material was published that threatened the foundations upon which the whole of our ministry to children was based. This was research by Dr Ronald Goldman who was a lecturer in Educational Psychology at the University of Reading in England.

It is impossible to write at length here on the content of this research and I must be satisfied with a summary statement. Goldman's research method was to play tape recorded Bible stories to children and then, through a series of questions, try to discover what ideas the child had derived from these stories. From their answers he concluded that 'the Bible is not a children's book'.

In his book *Readiness for religion* Goldman wrote,

> Bible teaching is an inadequate content for religious teaching, since it asks too much from the child and does not involve enough of his experience to make it relevant or sensible.

Statements such as this caused considerable concern to those of us who were committed to children's ministry and in the defence of our position numerous booklets and papers were produced in the latter part of the sixties. Dr Goldman's method of research was seen to be suspect, as was pointed out by Mr Reginald Hill, then editor of Scripture Union's Sunday School lesson materials, in a paper entitled *Can children understand the Bible?*

> It seems fair to comment ... that what he [Dr Goldman] discovered was the impossibility of understanding the material without good teaching—not, as he argues, the impossibility of giving successful teaching on this material.

On the positive side, this controversy caused us to examine

carefully the basis upon which our work was grounded. A further quotation from Reginald Hill reveals the direction in which Scripture Union was to move in the future.

> Since we accept the Bible as God's revelation of himself, we shall see it as our business to teach the Bible rather than something labelled 'Religious Education'. As we do so we must be willing to acknowledge that we have often been too slow to ask, 'What can this mean to these children?' and too ready to accept slip-shod answers. We must recognise, too, that the mere retelling of any Bible story is not enough. We must have before us a truth that arises quite naturally and directly out of the story, and we must be at pains to make this truth clear and relevant to their own experience.

This is an important principle that we must always keep in the forefront of our minds.

The greatest controversy of recent decades which seems to have been restricted to the Sydney scene, concerned the nature or content of the gospel. The debate began with a report of the Commission on Evangelism of the Church of England Diocese of Sydney under the title *Move in for action.*

The authors examined the content of the sermons in the book of Acts and asserted that the resurrection should be the principal focus of our preaching. Their conclusions can be summarised with the following quotation:

> Is it not striking that Paul does not refer to the death of Jesus as an atonement for sins in the synagogue nor does Peter, in any of his five addresses to Jews and God-fearers ever assert that salvation is connected with the death of Jesus.

In other words not one of the seven addresses of Peter and Paul recorded in Acts connects salvation with the death of Jesus.

The ensuing controversy came close to destroying Scripture Union's beach mission ministry. You can work with others who hold differing opinions on minor issues but when the debate concerns the content of the gospel message, the result is considerable strain.

While I was one who contended for the inclusion of the atonement as part of the message we were called to proclaim, I am conscious that the struggle left a legacy in my own thinking. I came to see that the resurrection of the Lord Jesus is an essential ingredient of the gospel. I am careful to continually remind those to whom I recount the message of the cross that Jesus' death was not the end of the story.

The following incident reported by one of our beach mission workers illustrates what I mean.

The worker in question was walking through the camping area inviting children to the mission meeting. One boy who had attended the previous day told him that he was not allowed to come to the mission any more. 'Well, if that's what your mother said, then that's what you must do.'

He was about to walk away when the boy said to him, 'Mister, was that the end of the story?'

'What do you mean?'

'They told us about this person called Jesus who was crucified even though he hadn't done anything wrong. It didn't seem fair to me.'

The mission worker realised that here was a child who had never heard the story before.

As you would expect the worker told the boy about the resurrection. The worker also approached the boy's parents and obtained their consent for him to attend the rest of the meetings.

All who preach the gospel must continually grapple with issues of this type. This is especially true for those who work with children. It has been well said that 'to teach simply you must know deeply.'

Never be satisfied with a collection of clichés when telling children the gospel.

Do your best to present yourself to God as one approved, a workman who does not need to be ashamed and who correctly handles the word of truth (2 Timothy 2:15).

Missions

Most of my time on the staff of Scripture Union has been spent conducting church based children's missions. Within a few weeks of my appointment to the staff back in 1954 I faced my first full scale after-school mission at an inner city Sydney church, Holy Trinity Erskineville. It now strikes me as incredible that at the time I had never been to an after school mission before. While I had had experience in beach mission and camps this was a whole new ball game. This mission was held over a period of two weeks and about one hundred and fifty children turned up each day. I was fully extended keeping control, let alone teaching them anything. To complicate life my second daughter Susan was born that week.

I attempted to take on far too much, arranging to speak at Scripture classes in various schools each morning in addition to the after school meetings. As a result, in the middle of the second week I croaked into the phone that I wouldn't be able to cope with Scripture that day. I had discovered that the voice box, like any muscle, performs best after it has been toughened up with constant use. Mine wasn't used to the sudden demand I was making on it.

A few years down the track I was better able to cope with a heavier speaking load. At Dorrigo I spoke to three school assemblies each morning followed by an after school meeting in the afternoon and an evangelistic meeting for adults at night. In addition I visited some smaller country schools at Deervale and

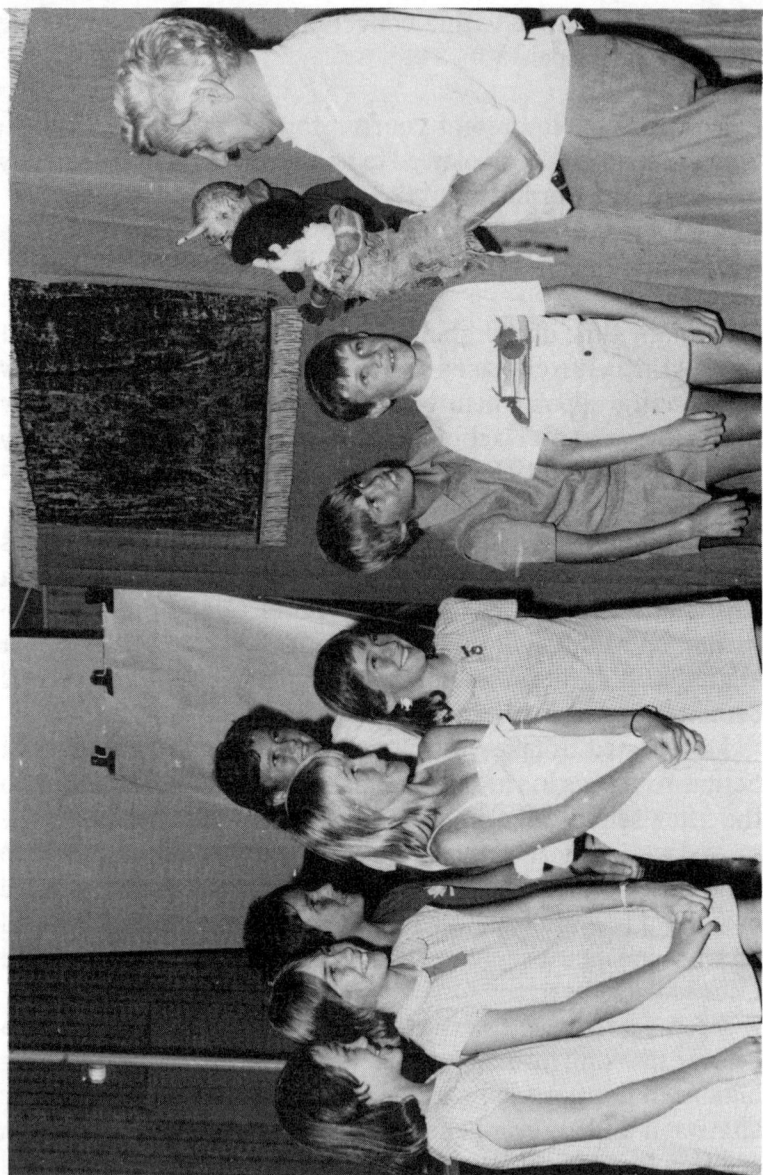

Cascade. A Rotary dinner and services on Sunday brought the total to forty nine meetings in nine days. While this is the heaviest engagement I can recall, many centres I visited put on a similar program.

Holiday clubs

'What do you know about Daily Vacational Bible Schools?' asked my friend Eric Walsham, the pastor of Wellington Baptist Church. Eric had invited me to the district a number of times to conduct after school missions. When I admitted that I had never even heard of a DVBS before, he explained that it was a new idea that had been developed in America.

'If I get you all the literature can you run one for me?' he asked.

As a result I led a VBS at Wellington each year for the next five years. I have participated in many similar ventures under the more suitable name of Holiday Bible Club. Through my involvement with holiday clubs I have come to recognise the value of regular itinerancy , by which I mean going back to the same centre each year for a number of years.

Millthorpe was one such centre that I visited frequently. We held a three hour program each morning for children and a teenage club for two hours each night. Having run the children's session for a couple of years we were not sure how the teen club would go but we decided to give it a try and waited expectantly the first night for a crowd to arrive.

A few young people wandered in, but the ranks were rather thin until a large group drifted past, perhaps curious to see what was going on. I recognised one of them from contact in previous years.

'Hi Jimbo! How's it going?' I called.

'Aw! Hi, Mr Shelley! Not bad.'

We were soon chatting like old friends while the rest of his gang stood around looking a bit sheepish.

'Righto you mob! We're going in!' announced Jimbo. Soon our program was rocking along and we had a 'full house' every night. In contacting teenagers I have always made the Jimbos my target, as these leader types have considerable influence within their groups.

Teenage holiday club programs have usually proved more successful in country towns, where most of the young people go to the same school, than in city suburbs where life is more impersonal. On the other hand children are very open to activity of this type. At a club with which I was involved recently, attendance peaked at one hundred and forty, which was all that we could comfortably handle.

The choice of location for a children's function is important; the nearer you hold an after school program to the school, the better. I enjoy watching children running excitedly down the road after school to attend a children's mission meeting.

At Gumly Gumly near Wagga on the first day of a week's mission it was raining 'cats and dogs'. The pianist and I sat waiting for school to finish, wondering whether any children would come. A car pulled up outside and a little girl alighted. I grabbed up my umbrella, saying, 'I'd better tell those folk not to leave that girl. It's unlikely that any others will come today.'

I hurried to the gate and to my astonishment saw a crowd of children running towards me through the rain. Few, if any, had coats. Most of them were soaking wet; yet all were chattering excitedly, eagerly anticipating the meeting. Such enthusiasm makes you want to produce your very best.

The smallest mission meeting I have ever held started with one child. Once again it was deluging with rain. Shortly after starting time one small boy put his head around the door.

'Is the meeting on?' he asked.

'Well you and I are the only ones here, but if you come in I will tell you a story,' I replied. A short time later three more children arrived and I carried on the program. Recently I met a woman who asked: 'Did you hold a mission meeting in Tempe about thirty years ago with only four children?'

'Yes! I certainly did! I remember it clearly!'

'I thought so,' she replied. 'I was one of those children!'

My experience has always been that children have very long memories. This is especially true of those who respond to the gospel message. A short time ago in Port Macquarie a woman asked me whether I believed that children could make an intelligent commitment to Christ. I replied that earlier in the day I had met a teacher at a local school who told me that she had put her trust in the Lord at a mission I conducted in Ballina 35 years before.

Although I have ranged far and wide throughout New South Wales over the years a large proportion of my time has been spent around Sydney, which absorbs a large proportion of Australia's migrant intake. As a result the children who attend functions such as after school missions, holiday clubs and the like are a very diverse group ethnically. We have a mission field in our own backyard. In the 1990's the need for children to hear and respond to the gospel is greater than ever.

The church is losing touch with the current generation of children. Often its activities for children are being conducted by 'grey power' as many of the younger people who could be taking the lead are reluctant to do so. This may be due partly to a lack of confidence. So I pray that some of the insights and techniques shared in *A to Z* will encourage and inspire others to give themselves to ministry with children, the most rewarding ministry there is.

ABSTRACT IDEAS

Experts in child development assert that children, especially small children, cannot grasp abstract concepts but think only in concrete terms. Francis Bridger advises those who teach infants (13 months to six years) to avoid teaching material which 'requires adult modes of thinking or logic. This rules out abstract concepts such as sin, salvation or redemption. It is highly unlikely that these can be recast in infant terms even if plenty of illustrations are used'.

For those of us involved with older children, the problem is not as acute but we must still be aware of it. The answer is to teach abstract concepts to children by starting with something concrete. Of course, knowing that children tend to take figurative language literally, we must take care when doing so. For example, to help children understand the abstract truth behind Jesus' statement, 'I am the door', we could proceed as follows.

What is a door?

It's a space in a wall that enables us to go from one room to another. We do not usually climb through the window unless we lose our keys. A door may be marked 'storeroom'. We go through this door if we want to find something we expect to be stored there. Another door may be marked 'Principal'. When we go through the door marked 'Principal', we expect to meet the Principal of the school. The door gives us access to the Principal's presence.

When Jesus said, 'I am the door' he didn't mean he was a hole in a wall or that he was made of wood. He meant that through him we could come to know and belong to God.

The above example moves from the concrete to the abstract in gradual steps. This is a hazardous journey at any time and requires careful thought and understanding of the capacities of children.

ACCOUNTABILITY

What is the position of the child in relation to God? Does there come a point when he or she becomes accountable to God? This question tends to be answered in one of two ways, so we can re-state it as follows.

Are all children lost until they make a conscious response to the gospel, or are infants safe because of their helplessness and lack of comprehension?

I can recall very vividly a conference of children's workers who were brought together to discuss this issue. I found the discussion so shattering that I wrote a paper, *The confessions of an ostrich*. In it I admitted to finding the question so difficult that my desire was to hide my head and attempt to ignore it.

Unfortunately this issue won't go away. It has provoked much heart searching over the years and it is still the subject of debate.

Some suggest that the age of accountability is twelve, arguing that this is when Jewish boys officially take on the responsibility of adulthood. They point out that the Lord Jesus was twelve years of age when he visited the temple and displayed considerable maturity as he sat amongst the teachers, 'listening to them and asking them questions'. (Luke 2:46–47). This suggestion appears speculative, however, when we consider the diversity of rates of development amongst children in general.

Between the wars, British Scripture Union evangelist, Montague Goodman used to say: 'We teach the lost condition of every child by nature, we believe that he needs to be saved'. He clarified this remark as follows:

> I know that the age of innocence is undoubtedly covered by Calvary ... The little innocent babe with no sense of responsibility or choice of good or evil is covered by Christ's atoning work at Calvary but the age of responsibility, of the choice of evil or good is reached and then comes the need.
>
> Not only in children is there early discovered a fallen nature and a rebel heart, but the fact is undoubted that *children left unrestrained will always grow up wicked*.

Notice that Goodman speaks about both an 'age of innocence' and an 'age of responsibility'.

This issue is also discussed by Dr Griffith Thomas in his book *Principles of Theology*, an exposition of the 39 Articles (or statements) of Anglican belief. Thomas says that little children are guilty of sin but that this is covered by the atonement, because they are incapable of sinning as an act of will. Thus little children are not subject to God's wrath. So Goodman (the member of a Brethren assembly) and Thomas (an Anglican) are in fact saying the same thing: infants are in a state of innocence prior to entering an age of accountability. Unfortunately neither of them provide scriptural backing for their statements.

In the late 1960's, John Pridmore wrote a thesis on *The New Testament Theology of Children'* for his M.A. degree. In it he drew attention to the Lord's statement in Mark 10:13–16: 'Let the little children come to me, and do not hinder them for the Kingdom of God belongs to such as these.' Pridmore pointed out that the phrase 'to such as these' is all-embracing, referring not only to the children who were brought to the Lord on that occasion but to all others like them. After discussing a variety of views on the reason for the children's acceptance, Pridmore concluded that small children are accepted by God 'because they are weak and helpless'. His views opened up considerable discussion and led to the publication of a number of books.

John Prince, in his book *Whose is the Kingdom* (now out of print), appears to dismiss Pridmore's proposition somewhat sweepingly yet he arrives at a similar conclusion.

> The conviction that all children are within the Kingdom until they opt out can be supported on more solid grounds than the dubious interpretation of a single Bible verse. Many evangelicals both as parents and as children's workers have based their actions on that conviction because it accords with what they know of the character of God.
>
> How could the God of the Bible, truly just, gracious, loving and merciful as he is, condemn a newborn infant incapable of expressing right or wrong?
>
> It is inconceivable. But if that is so, what about a one year old toddler, or a three year old, or ...?

Prince has in fact brought us back to the question of the age of accountability.

In his book *Children and God* (Scripture Union, 1988), Ron Buckland asks:

> Is there a moment in time, before which a child is not accountable to God and after which he is accountable? I believe the answer is a clear "No".

He continues:

> As he grows and develops, a child is increasingly accountable to God. We teach the gospel and nurture the child knowing that belongingness may become rebellion.

In response to all these questions and theological explorations, some people ask, 'What does it matter? Surely we should just get on with the job of telling children about the Lord Jesus!'

To some extent they are right—this is what we must do; but unfortunately it isn't as simple as that! Our belief about children and their accountability affects our approach to evangelising them.

My own conviction, based upon experience and consideration of such opinions as those of Pridmore and Prince (both of whom I believe have something useful to say) is that there *is* an 'age of innocence'. On this basis, I can reassure a parent who loses a child in infancy that their child is not rejected by God. Once we accept that there is an 'age of innocence' it follows that there must come a stage in a child's life when a child becomes accountable. While I recognise that it is impossible to select any specific age limit and state categorically that a child who has reached it is fully responsible for their own eternal destiny, my concern is more with how we approach the child and what we need to share of the gospel at different stages of development.

I believe there are three important things that children need to know.

1. The first issue we should be clear about is the reality of a child's sinfulness—a serious reality that all human beings must face. Fortunately children, in my experience, are pretty realistic and can readily recognise this truth. For example ask any class to suggest signs that people can't trust each other and they have no difficulty in compiling a lengthy list.
2. Next we must be clear that the Lord Jesus came into the world to deal with the problem of sin. If we portray him only as the one who is our great example we miss the very heart of the gospel.
3. The children we teach need to understand that our response to the Christian message affects the way we live.

ADVERTISING

The Salvation Army invited me to conduct a children's meeting as part of a mission in the Sydney suburb of Marrickville. At the time the army's training college was located in Marrickville and a number of army officers lived in the area as well. Sandy was the officer I liaised with in planning the mission. We chatted together about putting posters in the windows of local shops to advertise the meetings.

'Leave it with me!' announced Sandy. 'Marrickville is our town, we own the place. The Army is a very big customer. There isn't a shop in the district that would refuse to help us.'

In the days before our week of meetings, signs appeared in the windows of many of the local shops, reading: 'Boys and girls, ask inside for your free pass to the Whatchamacallit show'. Over three hundred children turned up on the first day.

When organising functions in a town or suburb, list all the ways that are available for advertising the event, e.g. contacts through Sunday schools, children's clubs, school classes, local radio, free suburban newspapers.

When you advertise a function for children, always clearly identify the organisation you represent. We are very prone to criticise other groups for failing to identify who they are, and yet we often forget this ourselves.

I frequently address school assemblies where I invite the children to attend after-school meetings. 'The meetings will be held at the Uniting Church and everyone is invited but you can only come of Mum or Dad says it's OK! Make sure you go home first to get your parents' permission.'

As well as indicating whom you represent, you should also be open about your purpose. I say to assemblies: 'If you come, I know you will enjoy it. There'll be games and competitions and quick sketch stories and puppets and afternoon tea but don't let me try to fool you, the main purpose is to tell you about the Lord Jesus, who he is and what he has done for you!' If your frankness turns anybody away, this must be accepted as the price of being truthful.

People in the community are understandably concerned for the safety and well being of their children. Publicity leaflets therefore should always state clearly the starting and finishing time of programs. A phone number for enquiries is useful as this enables them to check you out.

When putting together your promotion plans, don't overlook the ideas that the children themselves can offer. A suburban Sunday school invited me to speak at a guest morning. The children were asked to bring a friend to 'Sunday school with a difference' plus some goodies for a special morning tea. There were fifteen new faces at Sunday school that day.

A group of Christians at Warragamba organised an after-school club and asked the children to give their club a name. The suggestion they came up with was 'Kids Incorporated,' which certainly beats 'Happy Hour' or 'Adventure Time'—titles that have obviously been invented by adults.

As times have changed, so have the advertising tools I have used. Previously I used promotional blotters, but these became obsolete when ball-point pens were invented. Free tickets can be distributed with the captions 'Admit two to. . .'. Colouring competitions stimulate enthusiasm, and banners, posters, stickers and leaflets are all useful, but the strongest influence is the enthusiasm of the team!

AIMS IN STORYTELLING

The most important task in the preparation of a children's talk is to define clearly your aim. As any shooter will tell you, if you don't know what you're aiming for you won't know whether you hit it!

What is your purpose? First let me suggest what it is not!

(a) Your purpose isn't to teach geography

There may be some geographical information in your teaching but your primary purpose isn't to familiarise your pupils with the geography of the Holy Land, the way things were in Bible times, or the sequence of places visited by Paul on his missionary journeys.

(b) Your purpose isn't to teach history

Our teaching is based upon historical events. We will be eager to help our pupils recognise that this is so and that we are not merely telling myths and legends which have no historical basis. Nevertheless if we only succeed in communicating who did what and where and when, we have failed to achieve our basic purpose. Biblical knowledge has little value if taught for its own sake.

(c) Your purpose isn't to teach morality

If our primary purpose isn't to impart biblical knowledge or to teach history, geography or morality, what is it?

Our purpose is to proclaim the gospel. Immediately this gives rise to the question, 'What is the gospel?'

Paul sums up the gospel for us in 1 Corinthians 15:3 as follows:

What I received I passed on to you as of first importance: that Christ died for our sins according to the scriptures, that he was buried, that he was raised on the third day. . .

If we were to attempt to sum up our message in one word it would surely be 'Jesus'. Another way to define the gospel is 'God's good news to a guilty world'. It is good news for bad people.

Determine the aim of a lesson

While I may be clear in relation to my overall aim, the real difficulty arises when I am confronted with my particular class or group of children. 'If you aim at nothing you are sure to hit it.' Choose one clear teaching point for your talk, then plan your talk to communicate that teaching point. Resist the temptation to make additional points.

Your choice of teaching point will of course depend on the children in your particular group. How much do they already know? Are they from unchurched families or are they part of the church? For most of my life I have had an itinerant ministry. My practice is to ask as many questions as possible about the group I am to address, for example:

- How many children are in the group?
- What are their ages?
- Are they regulars at the club or Sunday school? and so on.

Questions such as these enable you to decide where to place the emphasis of your message. If you work regularly with a group you should have a greater understanding of their needs, but be on guard lest you lose sight of your aim and lapse into teaching geography, history or morality. If you teach from a prepared syllabus, recognise that it is easy for lesson book compilers to fall into the same trap.

Select a single aim

With most audiences, whether they are children or adults, a single aim is likely to be more successful. These days with powerful TV communication (especially in advertisements and music videos), people are becoming used to the single shot message.

In researching your biblical material you may find that several important and legitimate messages emerge from the story. They all may belong there and they all may be attractive to you as themes to explore in your talk. However, beware of confusing your audience. (This 'sin' is almost as bad as that of boring them!)

So choose your particular aim. Try to select the major theme or lesson that emerges from the biblical narrative, then craft the talk around it. It is helpful to write your theme or message down in one simple sentence then carefully work all the material so that the message emerges clearly.

For example, if you wanted to use the story of Jacob and Esau in Genesis chapters 25 and 32 for older audiences, you might decide to explore the biblical doctrine of propitiation. After describing Jacob's deceit and Esau's violent threats move quickly to the account of Jacob's return home twenty years later, Genesis 32, skipping over all the information relating to Jacob contained in chapters 26-31 as this is not relevant to your purpose on this occasion. Place your emphasis on Jacob's intention to pacify his brother's anger with an elaborate gift (Genesis 32:29).

With a younger audience however, you might wish to use the same story to illustrate the more straightforward theme of reconciliation. You could begin with a lively story of a child having a disagreement with a friend.

Clearly storytelling is a *craft*. It requires plenty of thought, careful research and understanding of the audience. You don't need me to tell you that writing usually requires more perspiration than inspiration! Ask any advertising copy-writer.

Make your teaching relevant

Have you ever heard someone address a group of children and use such examples as exceeding the speed limit or cheating on your tax return? Most of what we say to children is quite irrelevant to their experience of life. Stories and illustrations only enhance our teaching if they are appropriate.

To stay in tune with the world of today's boys and girls is a very valuable skill. You can't get it from books!

Correctly handle the word of truth

When I started work as a children's missioner I was a very raw recruit. At first my approach was to copy the style of older workers who had been in children's ministry for a number of years. Unfortunately there was a tendency among them to base much of their teaching on analogy, which I later came to recognise as not being the best way to teach children. One incident is clear in my mind.

It was breakfast time at Evans Head beach mission. In conversation with some of the team, I admitted I hadn't prepared the talk on the Good Samaritan that I was scheduled to give that morning.

'I guess I will have to fall back on an outline that I heard someone else give,' I said, 'even though it has nothing to do with the real meaning of the parable.'

'What do you mean?' asked Lenore, one of the group.

I replied that the outline made three points using the letters A, L, S. The speaker equated the injured man on the roadway with 'a lost sinner', the Samaritan was like 'a loving Saviour', and as a result the rescued man became 'a live Saint'.

'What's wrong with that?' Lenore asked.

'It has nothing to do with who our neighbour is, which was what Jesus was teaching through the parable,' I said.

'Well,' said Lenore, 'I can't see what's wrong with it, but if you can, you should not use it in that way!'

I excused myself from the meal and headed for the solitude of the sand dunes to prepare a talk focused on the message that the Lord intended the parable to teach.

If we rely on an analogy to teach a Bible story, we will miss the central truth in that story. Ultimately this undermines our efforts to teach the gospel. You will know you are switching to an analogy the moment you use the phrase, 'This is like. . .'.

We tend to resort to analogy when we are anxious to impress our hearers with the importance of making an immediate response to our teaching or to show that a Bible story is relevant to their lives. Such aims can also lead us to interpret Bible stories in quite fanciful ways. The parable of the Good Samaritan again comes to mind as an example; the following dialogue is from a play based on the parable.

Innkeeper: You've done a wonderful thing for this man. Why did you stop to help him when others walked past?

Samaritan: I'm a Christian and I read my Bible every day and it teaches me to help others.

Innkeeper: If reading the Bible did that for you, I'd better begin to read my Bible too.

Clearly the writer of this play wants to drive home the importance of Bible reading and hopes that the audience will be eager to go home and begin this good habit. Like the analogies mentioned in the story above, this application ignores the parable's central message, which is an answer to the question 'Who is my neighbour?'

ANIMATE YOUR PRESENTATION

To give a good children's talk you must be enthusiastic about your message and you must deliver it with verve. This is not a trick but an attitude. Of course, good delivery requires more than a positive attitude. Make sure that you exploit fully your natural attributes, e.g. the tone of your voice and the expression on your face, to get your message across.

Below I outline a couple of methods which contribute to an animated presentation.

1. Dramatic speech and action

King Belshazzar's feast, as related in Daniel 5, is one of the most dramatic moments in the whole of the scriptures. We read that while the nobles of Babylon were feasting, the fingers of a human hand appeared and wrote on the plaster of the wall. When he saw it the king's mouth dropped open [suit your expression to the statement]. He stared in amazement as the letters of the mysterious message appeared.

'Wha . . .wha . . .wha . . .what's happening?' he stammered.
'Wha . . .wha . . .what does this mean? Quickly!' he shrieked.
'Call the enchanters and the astrologers, find someone who can explain this. . .this. . .eh. . .m. . .mm. . .message!'

The scriptures tell us that 'The king's face turned pale and he was so frightened that his knees knocked together and his legs gave way.' You can try to convey the king's terror by using stammering speech and pointing with a trembling hand. It's a little more difficult to make your knees knock but you can try!

The aim of using dramatic speech and action is of course to bring alive for your hearers the emotions felt by the characters. To do this you must first develop a feel for the characters. For example, I was asked by a Sunday school to give a demonstration lesson on the set lesson in the series they were using. The lesson was based on prayer and the story used to illustrate it was that of Abraham's servant seeking a wife for Isaac. My first reaction was despair. How could I give a lesson to a group of nearly one hundred children from such an uninteresting story? Everything was so slow moving. There was no action that could be dramatically re-enacted.

I worked through the text with care, underlining all reference to the changing emotion of Abraham's servant. As I did so I began to feel something of the emotional struggle that he went through. Right from the outset he was apprehensive, asking Abraham, 'What if the woman is unwilling to come back with me?' (Genesis 24:5.)

Verse 12 records his prayer and in verse 15 we read 'before he had finished praying'. No wonder he was so astonished when, on requesting a drink from Rebekah, she offered to draw water for the camels as well. In passing it is interesting to note that after a long journey a camel will drink as much as twenty gallons of water. There were ten camels so Rebekah had quite a job on her hands satisfying their thirst. As she was involved in this task we read verse 21, that 'without saying a word, the man watched her closely', probably overcome with astonishment that his prayer had been answered so promptly. When he asked her which family she was from, and she had all the right credentials, he was so overcome that he fell flat on his face and had a one man praise session, verse 26.

At Rebekah's home her family extended a warm welcome, offering lavish hospitality, but the servant was so full of the astonishing sequence of the events that he had experienced that he refused to eat until he related what had happened. It is interesting to notice that in his account he referred to the emotions he felt as the events unfolded, verses 39, 45 and 48. In response to his story the family agreed that Rebekah could be Isaac's bride. This brought a further emotional outburst of gratitude from the servant as once again 'he bowed down to the ground before the Lord' verse 52.

In verse 54 we see him relaxed and at ease as they ate, drank and settled down for the night. Next morning he was eager to return home but his hosts were reluctant for Rebekah to leave so soon. As I studied the story I sensed his apprehension welling up again as he protested at being detained. It must have given him considerable satisfaction when later, on his arrival home, he 'told Isaac all he had done' (verse 66).

We must remember too that while Rebekah's reactions to these events aren't as easy to identify, she was not a passive participant in this drama. When Abraham's servant asked her for a drink her response was instantaneous as she 'quickly lowered her jar', verse 17. I see a hint of excitement in her movements as she emptied her jar into the trough and *ran* back to the well to draw more water. What thoughts went through her mind as the man gave her a gold nose ring and two gold bracelets? She must have had some realisation of what was afoot. This type of thing didn't happen every day!

Her words expressed eagerness as she informed the man that he would be welcome at their home, verse 25. Her excitement showed as the story tells that she *ran* and told her mother's household about these things', verse 28. There seems to have been no hesitation on her part when asked 'Will you go with this man?' (verse 57).

Bring the narrative to life!

'Never state a fact if you can bring it to life.'

The Bible records that when David went to meet the giant he was armed only with his sling and 'five smooth stones'. You could baldly state this fact to your audience or alternatively you could bring it to life by pretending to be David as he carefully selected those stones—picking up an imaginary stone and discarding it because it was either too flat or too rough or too light, then placing another in an imaginary pouch because it had the smooth surface he was looking for. If you do this, you are in fact enacting this part of the story very much the way it must have happened. It is legitimate to fill in some details in the Bible story using your imagination so long as what is said falls into the category of probability.

2. Sound effects

Clifford Warne was for many years the director of Anglican Television in Sydney. When he first started as a storyteller, he told the Jungle Doctor story of 'The goat that wanted to become a lion', wherever he went. I used the same story with a class in Newcastle, thinking it unlikely that Clifford would range so far. As chance would have it, a short time later Clifford visited Newcastle and told the same story to that same class. On returning to Sydney, he said, 'What do you mean by telling my story to a class in Newcastle?' 'Why, what happened?', I enquired. 'A little boy came up to me at the end of the period and said, 'Mr. Warne, you can't roar like Mr. Shelley can!' I suspect Clifford's roar was more realistic but mine would have exceeded it in volume.

It is difficult to explain the use of sound effects in writing, as sounds are difficult to write down and we can end up with the equivalent of a Batman comic with its 'wham', 'bam', 'zap' and 'bop' captions. Despite this limitation, it is worth mentioning that most children's speakers use descriptive sound effects. For example, when David's stone went 'clunk' against Goliath's forehead, the giant staggered back and went 'neeeenowww-vump' on the ground.

The purpose of these sound effects is to help your story live. Be careful not to overdo it, however; any sound effect, expression or gesture that draws attention to itself will detract from, rather than enhance, the effectiveness of your talk.

(See also p. 181 *Words that captivate* and *Dialogue in storytelling*)

BEGINNING A CHILDREN'S TALK

If you want to be effective as a communicator of God's good news, there's no point starting tentatively. You need to *arrest* people's attention. If you could x-ray the minds of an average audience, you would find people wandering along all kinds of pathways! The way to prevent this wandering is to appeal to their curiosity right at the start.

There are several ways to do this. These are:

1. *A question*

Direct questions are those to which you expect an answer, e.g. If you saw someone with a white walking stick what would you know about him? Rhetorical questions require no answer, e.g. If you saw someone with a white walking stick you would know they are blind wouldn't you? Either question could then lead into the story of blind Bartimaeus. (Be careful about using rhetorical questions with children. They usually try to give you an answer!)

Questions can be used to arouse the curiosity of your audience. 'I've got something in my pocket that is alive. What do you think it is?' After a series of guesses from the children, the speaker can produce a seed and then launch into a lesson on the parable of the sower.

2. *A brief story about another child (or children)*

This can either be true or imagined (be sure to tell your audience which it is). It may be an incident from your own childhood—but be careful not to exaggerate. Here is an example.

Bill had a new tennis racket and was enjoying hitting a ball against the wall of his house.

'Don't play there son, you might break the window,' warned his mother.

Despite her warning Bill continued to play and. . . smash, the ball went straight through the glass.

Bill dropped the racquet and ran and hid. Later when it began to get dark he slowly made his way home, very upset. To his surprise his mother hadn't discovered the broken window. When she saw his distress she comforted him instead of punishing him.

This introduction can lead into a talk about separation and reconciliation.

3. *Something topical*

Here is an example.

Who saw the television program about volcanoes on 'The world around us'? It showed people in Hawaii throwing fruit and vegetables into a volcano. They thought the mountain was a god and that the mountain must be angry with them. They were giving their god a gift to pacify him.

You could lead on to a biblical illustration of propitiation, e.g. Abigail seeking to pacify David's anger with a gift of food or Jacob sending livestock to his brother Esau to smooth the way for his home-coming.

4. *Start straight in to tell a Bible story*

When planning to recount a Bible story, ask yourself, 'Where shall I begin?' The best place to start is *not* the beginning of the story but towards the end—in fact, as close to the end as possible. Confused? Look at the following example.

Goliath the giant muttered to himself as he strapped on his heavy helmet and picked up his enormous spear.
'This is becoming ridiculous!' he grumbled.
'I've been challenging these chicken-hearted Israelites to send out a champion to fight me every day for the past month. There's no chance that any of them will have a go. Still I'd better do what the captain wants.'
The Philistine champion lumbered over to the edge of the valley and after taking a deep breath, began to shout.
'Hey! Over there! Send out someone to fight me. If he can beat me, we will be your servants but if I beat him, then . . .'
'What? Don't tell me someone is coming! I don't believe it!'

This introduction has the following features:
(a) It introduces the antagonist early so that we know what the protagonist, i.e. the hero, is up against. This is an important

technique in building up suspense. In the story of David's battle it's easy to identify the antagonist, but who or what is the antagonist in the story of Naaman?

(b) It plunges into the action: the moment of combat is only moments away. The effect is much more gripping than it would be if the storyteller started back at David's home and laboriously described him making his way to the battlefront. (It is best to bring in that information as a flashback).

(c) It uses a good deal of dialogue, which has a fascination for the listeners.

(d) It uses colourful language e.g. muttered, grumbled, lumbered.

(e) It uses an interrupted line or a pause: 'if I beat him, then. . .'

I cannot stress too strongly the importance of planning a good introduction. It has been truly said that 'Well begun is half done.'

BEHAVIOUR

Mix together hot weather, 300 children, no amplification, and unsuitable visuals and you have a recipe for chaos. Chaotic would be the only way to describe an after school mission I conducted in Tempe, an inner city suburb of Sydney. Attendances at these meetings exceeded three hundred every day, all my pre-prepared visuals were far too small and without amplification, it was a struggle to be heard above the din.

The original plan was to conduct the mission for eight school afternoons, concluding on the Wednesday of the second week, but after the first few days the misbehaviour was so bad that it seemed pointless to continue. I discussed the problem with the

minister and arranged to extend the mission for the full fortnight. The Monday of the second week was for 'boys only', on
Tuesday it was the girls' turn, and so on. In this way we were
able to reduce the crowd to a more manageable group. We
rearranged the hall as much as possible, setting out the chairs
in angled instead of straight rows and changing the lay-out of
the platform. This meant that the children came into a different
situation rather than the one that had become associated in
their minds with a riot.

I worked till late at night preparing larger visuals that all
would be able to see and I arrived early each day to ensure that
everything was in readiness for the session. We also tightened
up our control methods, lining the group up at the door and
bringing them in in an orderly fashion instead of permitting a
wild rush. The front seats were kept for the smaller children
who can be disruptive if seated further back where they cannot
see. The program started briskly and it moved smoothly and
rapidly from one item to another.

The difference that these simple changes made was dramatic.
The first week of that mission was agony, the second week a delight.

'Please sir, may I go to the toilet?'

Whenever I conduct an after-school children's mission or a kids
club I give my helpers four instructions:
(a) Show the children where to leave their school bags.
(b) Record their names and addresses.
(c) Indicate where they should line up for afternoon tea.
(d) Remind them to go to the toilet.

Failure to remember this last instruction can cause havoc if
the please-may-I-go-to-the-toilet bug hits halfway through a
session. If one child asks to go, you can be certain that others
will want to follow.

'If you poke a stick in a beehive. . .'

Anyone experienced in handling bees will know that it is unwise to stir them up. The same principle applies to large groups of children, as the following example shows.

'Hullo, boys and girls!' shouted the beach service leader.

'Hullo!' they replied.

'What? I can't hear you!' shouted the leader.

I needn't tell you that after a few more exchanges of this type, the children at that meeting reached screaming pitch. That leader soon found that it was much more difficult to settle them down than it had been to start them up. By all means lead with enthusiasm, but avoid this type of pointless whipping up.

Throughout the program, control must come from the platform. Nothing undermines the meeting more than some well meaning helper chiming in and scolding children for inattention. The leader must be aware of the trouble spots in the audience and deal with them promptly.

It is important to be entirely impartial towards all of the children. Avoid any sexist or racist remarks. If a child is particularly disruptive and you have no success with moderate methods of control, such as eye contact as you are speaking, then ask him to move to a seat close to the door. In doing so explain that if he continues to misbehave you will have to ask him to leave.

The advantage of this approach that if you do find it necessary to send the child home, there is less disruption than if he clambers out over the feet of a row of children. If you do have to take the final step and dismiss the offender, it is essential to do so without heat. I would say, 'I'm terribly sorry to have to ask you to leave, but for the sake of all the others who want to enjoy our meeting I'll have to do so.'

Fortunately, there have been very few occasions over the years that I have had to dismiss any of the children.

'Coming the heavy'

When I was still a teenager and newly converted from a non-church background I was severely reprimanded by a clergyman for lax behaviour in 'the house of God'. A group of us were removing Christmas decorations and I had clambered up a metal stanchion to remove some streamers. I admit that I may have been showing off a bit to some of my friends but the vehemence with which I was ticked off left a lasting impression on my mind. I have seen similar things happen to others since. At an after school club that I visited the children were fidgeting and giggling, and the leader, in his exasperation, began to pray very loudly that Satan (who was so obviously present) would be rebuked.

Having prayed, he then berated the children for this misbehaviour in 'the house of God'. In fact, much of their bad behaviour was the result of his own incompetence as a leader. He had commenced the meeting with a boisterous chorus that stirred them up and while they were singing he left the platform to chat to another of the leaders.

The benefit of the doubt

Some of us unconsciously build up a defeatist attitude towards individual children who prove to be difficult. Yet the misbehaviour may have causes that we know nothing about. One young teacher of my acquaintance was having a lot of difficulty controlling a boy in her class. Later when she discovered that the boy's rebelliousness was partly due to a family break-up in his home, her attitude of antagonism changed and as a result he responded much more positively.

Personal check list

If I have a troublesome session at a club or assembly or mission program, I try not to excuse myself by blaming the children. From experience I know that the first thing to do is check my own performance.

1. Was I too busy to prepare properly?
2. Was I too tired? Was I enthusiastic?
3. Were the theme and the program uninteresting?
4. Was the tempo of the program too slow?
5. Was I alert enough to what was happening in the group? Was I flexible?
6. Did I 'capture' the attention of the children from the first moment?
7. Did I adequately brief the other members of the team?

The smooth running of a children's program depends on many things, but the most influential one is. . . you!

(See *Understanding children*)

BIBLE READINGS

It is difficult to hold the attention of children with a Bible reading during a meeting. If a Bible reading is included in your program, it is helpful to alert the children beforehand to a question you intend to ask when the reading is over.

Some family services include a dramatised reading with various readers taking part. This helps to capture audience attention. Another option is to illustrate your story-telling using an overhead projector transparency with overlay figures that are moved in by an assistant.

In ministering to adults it is common to read the Bible passage first and then to go back over it and explain it. This is not good practice for the children's worker; if you read the story beforehand, the children will know how it ends, and thus you have 'stolen the meat off the dish.'

When invited to speak at a family service or similar function where a reading from the Scripture is the accepted procedure, rather than reading the story about which I intend to speak, I select a passage that has a similar emphasis.

BOOKS FOR CHILDREN'S WORKERS

Yes! Others have been there before you and they have had to grapple with the problems you are facing. Fortunately they have made their insights available in books. Here are some I've found useful.

Here's help (Christian Education Publications) gives brief insights into the characteristics of each of the age groups that we categorise as childhood. This knowledge has many practical applications; for example you will be able to avoid using concepts and language that are beyond the understanding of your particular group.

Help! There's a child in my church: working with 7–11s by Peter Graystone (Scripture Union UK) encourages and enables you to make children part of the church family.

Under fives welcome: working with under fives in church by Kathleen Crawford (Scripture Union UK) is the companion volume for those working with very small children.

Children finding faith by Francis Bridger (Scripture Union UK) discusses some of the difficulties we confront when we try to communicate spiritual concepts to children.

Puppet drama: a complete illustrated guide by Robert and Jill French (Scripture Union Australia). The cover reads 'with Owen Shelley' so obviously I am keen to promote it! This book is the culmination of many years of experimentation with puppets in children's ministry. It provides valuable information that will enable you to attain a higher level of proficiency than if you started out on your own. (See *Puppets* for an outline of the contents of this book.)

That they may learn: towards a Christian view of eduction (Lancer Books). Brian Hill is Professor of Education at Murdoch University W.A. In this book he shows how biblical insights about teachers, learners and the content of education challenge present-day assumptions. He also discusses the politics of promoting educational change.

Read aloud Bible stories Volumes 1, 2, and 3 by Ella Lirdvall (Moody Press). These books contain Bible stories for pre-school children. These are exceptionally good products that can be highly recommended to the parents of the children you teach.

Children & God by Ron Buckland (Scripture Union Australia). Recently we have seen some books published which explore the nature of a child's faith. Of these, Ron Buckland's book should be read by everyone who is serious about children's work. Buckland looks at what the Bible says about Jesus' attitude to children and their place in God's whole plan for his church and his world.

Telling stories to children by Marshall Shelley (Lion). Most of the books on storytelling that I have found helpful are now unfortunately out of print. However *Telling stories to children* is still available.

BORN AGAIN

A friend of mine was asked, 'Are you a born again Christian?'
She wisely replied, 'What other kind is there?'
I groan inwardly when I hear enthusiastic Christian workers telling children that they must be born again. My reason is that I am painfully aware that the children will be just as perplexed as was Nicodemus to whom the Lord Jesus first used the term. I am also aware that many of the workers do not understand it themselves, yet in some circles, to be able to claim to be a 'born again Christian' is a test of orthodoxy.

The Lord Jesus explained the term by stating 'No-one can enter the Kingdom of God unless he is born of water and the Spirit' (John 3:5).

In his book *Learning and living the Christian life* the Rev G R Harding Wood had this to say by way of explanation:

The language is pictorial. The word 'water' would mean 'cleansing' and the word 'Spirit' indicating the kind of cleansing. Jesus meant spiritual cleansing (see Titus 3:5).

The correctness of this interpretation is proved by the grammatical construction in the Greek original. It is an example of what is called *hendiadys*. The word literally means 'one in two', one thought expressed in two figures.

The two figures of speech used by Jesus are 'water' and 'Spirit'. The one thought expressed is—spiritual cleansing.

I have included this explanation for those who wish to teach the story of Nicodemus' interview with the Lord Jesus.

Mostly I avoid using the term 'born again' with children as even when you understand it, it requires a complicated explanation to get the meaning across. I prefer to encourage them to put their trust in the Lord Jesus as this is less obscure.

BREAKING THE ICE

One of the skills that the itinerant children's worker needs to develop is the ability to break the ice in making contact with groups of children who are strangers. A simple point of contact that I have used is to say to a child, 'Don't tell me your name. Tell me the first letter'.

'S.'

'Susan, Sarah, Samantha, Shelly, Sausage. . . Oops. . . no-one ever calls you Sausage, do they!'

I carry on in this vein until I discover the right name. By this time others in the group are eager for me to guess their names. Another trick is to guess the children's ages. After you have been doing this a while you usually come close to the right age every time.

(See *Names*)

CRUCIFIXION

Tell the story of the cross often. It has its own compelling power.

Below is an outline which focuses on the incidents surrounding the crucifixion in a slightly different way. It is suitable for older children who may think they know the story well. Viewing it from another angle can stimulate their interest.

You will need five large pictures of hands to illustrate the characters in the talk.

- Hand with money—Judas
- Hand holding message—Pilate's wife
- Hand washing—Pilate
- Hand nailed to log—Thief
- Hand pointing—Centurion

Talk outline

1. Introduction

You are standing outside the school waiting for the bus when 'screech, crash' [whatever sounds you can make] right in front of your eyes you see a huge truck smash into a little Corolla. Soon a police car arrives. When the police find out that you saw it all happen with your own eyes, they ask for your name and address.

You have become an eye witness and later you will be asked to attend the trial and tell what you saw. [Talk some more about eye-witnesses.]

There may, however, be other witnesses who were not present at the scene of a crime but are called to give testimony on behalf of the person who has been arrested. These are character witnesses.

2. Judas

At the time of the trial and crucifixion of the Lord Jesus a number of people made statements about his character. The difference is that none of these people could be described as his friends. [Show first picture—hand with money.] This one used to be. This is the hand of the disciple who betrayed Jesus. What was his name? Judas was bribed to betray the Lord Jesus to the Romans. How much money was he paid?

[Recount the incident of Judas returning the money from Matthew 27:3–5.]

When Judas spoke about Jesus he described him as 'innocent'. What does innocent mean? [Discuss this.]

3. Pilate's wife

The second witness is a very strange one. [Hold up the second picture—hand with letter.]

Pontius Pilate was the Roman Governor at the time of the trial of the Lord Jesus. As he was listening to the accusations that were made, the trial was interrupted by a messenger from his wife. Pilate had been asked to hold the trial of Jesus early in the morning. After he left, his wife tried to go back to sleep but her thoughts troubled her. Her feeling became so strong that she called for a servant and sent this message to her husband.

The message read, 'Don't have anything to do with that innocent man. I have had nightmares because of him' (Matthew 27:19 CEV).

Pilate's wife must have heard about the Lord Jesus, as she would be unlikely to describe him as 'innocent' otherwise.

4. Pontius Pilate

Pontius Pilate wasn't silly. [Show the third picture.] As he listened to the accusations that were made against Jesus, he realised that they were all false. Calling for a basin of water he washed his hands (Matthew 27:23–24). His verdict was 'I don't find this man guilty of anything' (John 18:38).

5. The thief

[Show the fourth picture. Although you would briefly report the conversation that followed between the thief and Jesus, remember that on this occasion the primary focus is not the conversation but the thief's testimony to the character of Jesus.]

6. The Army Captain

[Show the fifth picture and explain the role of the centurion.] His testimony is found in Luke 23:47 (CEV): 'Jesus must really have been a good man.'

7. You and me

Which one of us would be described by our enemies as innocent and good? Even our friends wouldn't say that about us. We have all been guilty of things like telling lies, cheating and being selfish or cruel or proud.

The good news is that through the death of Jesus, the one

who was innocent, we the guilty ones can be forgiven.

[You could conclude your lesson by quoting a relevant Bible verse, e.g. John 3:16 or Romans 5:8 or even giving an invitation to respond by praying a prayer of acceptance. See *Inviting a response*.]

CURIOSITY

When I was a very inexperienced club leader, the boys taught me many lessons about how to keep their attention. At first I mostly learned how difficult this was! It would be more accurate to describe our Friday night sessions as weekly riots rather than boys' club nights. One night I gained a valuable insight. We had arranged a talk by a missionary pilot who was about to leave for Papua New Guinea. His presentation was excellent and our wild bunch gave him their rapt attention. The memory of that night still makes its mark on my thinking.

In short, we don't win the interest of an audience unless we have something interesting for them to see and hear. Workers with children need to be wide awake enough to know what appeals to them. Identify the curiosity factor and build your teaching around it!

Some years ago I obtained a flan-o-graph of Patricia St. John's story, *Treasures of the snow*. Using it as a serial story at an after-school mission I concluded the first episode at the point where Lucien and Dani, two of the main characters, have a fight which results in Dani falling over a cliff. To my delight the first boy to arrive at the mission the following day greeted me with the words, 'I'll bet that kid didn't get killed!'

You will not be surprised that I used that flan-o-graph so constantly that I wore it out. In more recent years I have performed the same story as a serialised puppet play, having found that the story consistently stimulates the children's interest.

DIALOGUE IN STORYTELLING

If in the course of your storytelling you describe a character in terms of height, weight and even eye colour, your audience will still have little understanding of the type of person they are. It is through the use of dialogue that your audience are able to visualise characters in their imagination. Dialogue is a very effective tool and is worth using frequently. In some instances you need only to repeat the dialogue that occurs in the Bible text, while in others you must rely on your imagination.

A simple key to developing dialogue is to switch into speech the details that are reported in narrative form in the Bible passage. For example much of the account of the search by

Abraham's servant for a wife for Isaac is in narrative. Compare the following example of dialogue with Genesis 24.

'Mother, mother look what I've got!'
'What is it Rebekah?'
'A nose ring of gold and two golden bracelets!'
'What?' Where did you get them from?'
'From a man, a man I met at the well. He, he asked me for a drink and I gave him some of my water and drew water for his camels as well.'
'Was he by himself?'
'No! He had servants with him. He asked whether there would be room here at our house where they could stay. He asked my name and which family I belong to. When I told him he fell down on the ground and worshipped the Lord. He mentioned the God of Abraham!'
'Abraham! Here, quickly Laban, run and see who this fellow is who has given your sister these valuable presents. If he has come from Abraham you must invite him to our home at once!'

None of this conversation is recorded in scripture and yet it must be very close to what was said at the time when 'the girl ran and told her household about these things' (Genesis 24:28). When you change narrative into dialogue you heighten the interest of the story.

Another key to writing dialogue is repetition. For example in Elisha's time four leprous men return to the besieged city of Samaria with the news that the surrounding army had fled (2 Kings 7).

'Your majesty, your majesty! The gatekeepers have reported that some lepers came to tell us the enemy has fled.'
'It's a trap', thundered the King. 'The enemy know how weak

we are. They know we are starving. They have left their camp to hide in the hills in ambush. They think we'll rush down to their camp to get food and they'll be able to capture us alive and get into the city'.

'B-But your majesty, what if it's true? What if they really have gone?'

'No! No way! I'm awake to their little scheme. The enemy are hiding in ambush hoping we'll rush down to their camp and leave the city unguarded. They'll be able to capture us if we do that and get into the city.'

'Sir, just in case it is true, order some of the men to take five of the horses that are left and check it out—soon.'

Note that the King's speech from 2 Kings 7:12 is repeated. (See *Embellishment, Words*)

EMBELLISHMENT

It is important to lay a good foundation for children's understanding of the truths of the Bible. Sometimes we work against this by unnecessarily or inappropriately embellishing the details of Bible stories.

The events surrounding the birth of Jesus have suffered most in this respect. At an infants school assembly I attended, the speaker focused her entire address on the donkey that Mary rode to Bethlehem. There is no reference whatever to a donkey in the Gospels; very probably Mary walked all the way!

This problem is not confined to the Christmas story. Many a Sunday school lesson has been based on 'the boy who gave his lunch to Jesus'. Frequently he is portrayed as the most important person in the incident and his action is depicted as an example for others to follow. The Gospels, however, give him no such prominence. Only John's account mentions him in a brief phrase: 'Here is a boy with five small barley loaves and two fish'. While it is important not to overlook details that make the story live, this is an example of the other extreme of making too much of something minor.

I have frequently heard children's workers say, 'Jesus said. . .such and such. . . ' when there is no record of such a statement in the Gospels. They may be expressing ideas that are found in the epistles. Some will argue that because the epistles are the 'Word of God' we can attribute them to the Lord Jesus. I prefer to say 'Paul said,' or 'Peter said' rather than claim that the statement was made by the Lord himself. If we preached a sermon to adults and made an incorrect statement like this, someone would be sure to point out our error. Because the audience we are addressing are *only* children and are unlikely to notice, this does not give us license to put words into the Lord's mouth.

ENTHUSIASM

Enthusiasm is vital. Beware of being too 'laid back' or 'low key' in your approach.

Camp Conqueror was a bushwalking camp based at Milton on the south coast of NSW. The leaders of this camp had what I would call a 'second preference mentality'. Each year the camp failed to attract sufficient numbers of first choice applicants and so it had come to depend on the overflow of applicants from other camps to fill their numbers.

When I took over the leadership of the camp I set out to correct this negative attitude. To begin with I invented a slogan which we painted in large letters on the wall of the galvanized iron shed that functioned as our cookhouse: 'Conqueror, the camp with class'.

Next we examined together the program from previous years and planned a new schedule of activities. The team were somewhat taken aback when I repeatedly said, 'We can't do that! You did that last year!' I am not inferring that an entirely new program is appropriate in all cases, but I knew that this was what would breathe new life into Camp Conqueror.

I can still remember the moment the campers arrived. As they tumbled out of the bus I overheard one of them say, 'It hasn't changed! It's the same old place!' I knew that this was not meant to be a derogatory remark but I was determined to let them know that while it was 'the same old place' it was under new management. Introducing myself I told them how fortunate they were to have chosen to come to 'the best camp ever'. Looking back I wouldn't describe it as the quite like that. We had our problems and a number of the campers resisted the changes that I initiated. It took almost a week before some of them accepted my leadership.

Despite these difficulties, the following summer Conqueror was the first to fill its quota and we had to send some of the late applicants off to other camps.

ETERNAL LIFE

Many booklets published to help children trust and follow the Lord Jesus place considerable emphasis on heaven and how to get there. Their line of argument runs like this. 'Heaven is a wonderful place! You want to go to heaven don't you? You can't go to heaven if you are sinful. You need to be forgiven so that you can go to heaven.'

Please don't misunderstand me when I say that I prefer to think of heaven as a 'fringe benefit' rather than the central reason for making a response to the gospel. I place more emphasis on what the Lord Jesus can do for us now. We can enjoy his friendship, we can know his guidance and we can experience his help in overcoming sin in our lives. So can the children we try to reach. We cannot change the world but we can, with God's help, change individual lives.

Ask any group of children from a church background, 'What is eternal life?' and the answers you will get will all focus on 'living forever in heaven'. I say to them 'Yes, that's part of it.' This causes many a puzzled look, as generally children have not been taught that eternal life isn't only a question of quantity but also a matter of quality. This is a much more difficult concept to get across to children but don't let that daunt you. It is important that they learn it.

In explaining 'eternal life' I explain what 'eternal death' is. Romans 6:23 tells us that 'The wages of sin is death.' Death isn't merely dying in a physical sense. Spiritual death is to be separated from God, shut off from him. For this reason Paul describes our state prior to coming to know the Lord Jesus as being 'dead in trespasses and sins'. If spiritual death is to be separated from God then spiritual life must be the opposite i.e. belonging to God, being with him.

Eternal life means belonging to God now and always. Because I know that God is my friend, my life will be a better kind of life than when I try to live without him. This is a life with a purpose: to serve and please God here and now. The ultimate goal of this life is to be with him in his home, called heaven.

EYE CONTACT

As I mounted the pulpit of the small country church I discovered that my view of the congregation was completely obscured by a large vase of waratahs. Remembering from Bible college that, as God's messenger, I was the most important person there at that moment, I picked up the vase, and with comments of appreciation, moved it to a more appropriate place.

Clear eye-communication between the speaker and everyone in the group is essential. If something hinders clear communication with your audience, change it. If I notice that some of the children are sitting where I cannot see them, I unobtrusively ask one of the organisers to move them.

The following conversation with one of my sons took place when he was twelve.

Me: 'How did the school service go today son?'
Him: 'Ah—alright!'
Me: 'What did the speaker speak about?'
Him: 'Ah-I don't know!'
Me: 'Why don't you know?'
Him: 'I didn't listen.'
Me: 'Oh–why didn't you listen?'
Him: 'Aw—he was just like the others. They just get up and talk, they don't talk to you!'

If you don't give the impression that you are talking *to* them, the children in your group cannot be blamed if they switch off. When speaking, keep your head up, look towards the centre of the group and speak out clearly. Don't look at a fixed point somewhere in the distance above their heads—it is essential to give your audience the feeling that you are speaking personally to each one of them.

FAITH

Faith is frequently misunderstood. Faith is not a calculated risk, but a calculated certainty (see Hebrews 11:1). There are three elements to true faith: knowledge, belief and trust. Notice that faith is not a step in dark, but a step in the light—it is based on knowledge.

The following outline attempts to explain what faith is. I have selected one of the characters listed for us in Hebrews chapter eleven, but you could use any of the others mentioned in that chapter, or numerous New Testament characters to make the same point.

I use the knowing, believing, trusting outline with a variety of stories.

Talk outline

1. Promised gifts

Bill and Susan's father was leaving home to go on a business trip to Hong Kong.

'I'll only be away for two weeks,' he told them, 'and I'll see if I can bring you something nice when I come home.'

For the next two weeks they thought about his promise and wondered what he would bring. Imagine their excitement when the taxi arrived bringing their father home. They rushed to greet him. As well as his suitcases, there were a number of other parcels. They could hardly control their curiosity.

'Well my dear, here's a little something for you' said their father handing their mother a package. She opened it up. It was a new necklace.

'Thank you dear, it's lovely' said their mother.

'What did you bring for us?' asked Bill.

'Now what makes you think I've brought something for you?' teased their father.

'You promised!' said both of the children together. They knew that he had said he would bring something, they believed that he would keep his promise, they trusted his promise by asking for their gifts. They had faith in their father's word.

How pleased their father must have been to know they thought he could be trusted to keep his promises. God has made some promises to us. He has promised that we will be forgiven if we believe in the Lord Jesus. Do you think that God would break a promise?

2. Trusting Daddy

There's a story about a little girl who was looking for her father. When she called him, his voice came from down in a cellar (a room under the house). She looked down into the cellar but everything was pitch dark.

'Are you down there Daddy?' she asked.

'Yes dear, jump and I'll catch you!' replied her father.

'But I can't see you daddy!'

'But you can hear me and you know I can catch you. Jump, you will be quite safe!'

'Alright Daddy I'm coming!'

And she jumped!

Of course her father caught her easily. When he put her down she ran back up the steps and called 'Here I come again Daddy'.

She knew her father was there. She believed that he would catch her so she trusted him and jumped. She had faith in her father. The Lord wants us to put our faith in him. If you know about the Lord Jesus and believe that he is the Son of God, then trust yourself to him. That is, believe that he welcomes you to his family and that he has power to forgive the wrong in your life.

3. The spies on the roof

Back in early Bible times, a woman called Rahab became one of God's special people because she put her faith in God (Joshua chapter 2). Rahab lived in Jericho and everyday reports were coming in about the advancing Israelite army.

'The Israelites have defeated King Sihon. Not one of the cities of the Amorites have been able to hold out against them' reported one of the spies.

Rahab heard this report and thought about it: 'The God of these Israelites must be very powerful.'

'Og, King of Bashan has been conquered!' reported another spy. 'The Israelites have captured more than sixty cities even though the cities had strong walls and barred gates.'

'Why couldn't the gods of the Amorites protect them?' thought Rahab.

'They'll have to cross the Jordan river before they can attack us,' said someone hopefully.

'Bah! The river won't stop them. Haven't you heard how they crossed the Red Sea when they were escaping from Egypt? The waters rolled back and they marched through the empty sea bed!'

Rahab could see that all the people of Jericho were scared stiff. 'Those men, the strangers that have been staying at my house, I wonder if they are spies' she thought to herself. Quickly she hurried home.

In those days people believed that there were many different gods. Usually they expected their gods to be powerful in their own area. They trusted their gods to protect them from invaders but what Rahab had heard about the God of the Israelites was different. Their God helped them wherever they were. Rahab believed the reports she had heard and she made a bold decision to trust herself to the Israelites even though it meant betraying her own people.

'You are spies from the Israelite army aren't you?'

She seemed so certain that they didn't try to deny it.

'We have heard how the Lord dried up the waters of the Red Sea when you came out of Egypt. We have heard how your army has conquered Sihon and Og, the Kings of the Amorites. We know that your God has given you this land and we are all very frightened. Your God is very powerful. He is the God of heaven above and in the earth below. Please spare the lives of my family.'

'Our lives for your lives!' they agreed.

Rahab acted swiftly. [Describe her plan to hide the spies from the guards (Joshua 2:6).]

'Thump, thump, thump. The guards were hammering on the door.

'Open up in the name of the King' they ordered.

'I'm coming! Wait a minute! I'm not properly dressed' called Rahab as she stalled for time.

[Recite the conversation with the guards (Joshua 2:3-5). Describe the escape plan (Joshua 2:15-21).]

'We promise you will be safe' said the spies 'but you must be in this house. If anyone in your family leaves this house and goes out into the street he'll only have himself to blame. Tie this rope to the bars of your window so that we will know which house is yours.'

After making this promise the men slid down the rope and headed for the hills. [Briefly describe the events that followed (Joshua. 6:1–24).]

I wonder whether any of Rahab's family were frightened when they heard the noise of the battle.

'Rahab, are you sure we will be safe here?'

'Quite sure, so long as you stay in this house. The cord in the window is our protection!'

'But how do you know they will take any notice of it?'

'They promised we would be safe and I believe them'.

Rahab acted in faith. She knew about the God of Israel and because she believed he was the true God she trusted herself and her family to the mercy of the Israelites.

As a result she became a member of God's special people and her name is listed in the family tree of the Lord Jesus (Matthew chapter 1).

4.   Faith in Jesus Now

Many people know about Jesus but do nothing about it. Faith is knowing, believing and trusting. Listen as I read John 1:11–12. 'He came to his own country but his own people did not receive him. Some however did receive him and believed in him, so he gave them the right to become God's children.' When Jesus came many of the people did not believe him when he said that he was God's son. But those who welcomed him and believed in him became members of God's family. We can be part of God's family too, when we put our faith in him.

FINDING A NEW ANGLE

A friend who was teaching a class of junior teens asked me to help her prepare a lesson on the Palm Sunday coming of Jesus to Jerusalem. 'These kids have been to church since they were knee-high,' she said. 'They'll know it all—back, front and side ways!'

Together we examined all four narratives in the Gospels, desperate for a new angle on this familiar theme. I was grasping at anything. 'I wonder if Bartimaeus was there? A short time beforehand he was described as following Jesus.'

We could not assume Bartimaeus was in fact present, but we went on to ask who may have been there and we built a lesson around the idea of the reactions of people in the crowd. We found four groups.

1. People who didn't understand

They asked 'Who is this?' (Matthew 21:10).

2. People who knew who Jesus was

They had seen Lazarus being raised from death and this convinced them Jesus was the Son of God (John 12:17).

3. People who were annoyed

The Pharisees asked Jesus to silence the enthusiastic crowd (Luke 19:39).

4. People who were interested

The Greek onlookers requested an introduction to Jesus (John 12:20).

The new angle worked—my friend reported a successful lesson.

Then the trouble began! I told the above story to illustrate a point in a training session. 'That's great,' said a pastor .

' Now help me find another angle for the next Palm Sunday! Let's face it. I can't change churches just because I've run out of Palm Sunday talks!'

We worked on the theme again, beginning with the prophecy of Jesus about the overthrow of Jerusalem (Luke 19:41–44) and the subsequent fulfilment in AD 70. This could make a fascinating lesson for junior teenagers. Another angle you could explore would be to trace the effects that the events had upon Jesus' enemies. All the Gospel writers seem to mention it.

If you look carefully enough with eyes wide open, you'll find unusual angles in the familiar Bible narratives. But beware of such solutions as telling the Palm Sunday story from the point of view of the donkey! They rob you of the opportunity of treating Jesus and his claims seriously.

You need to be careful about mixing elements from the different Gospel accounts. Each Gospel writer prepared his story under God's inspiration to convey a particular point. It is always interesting, however, to compare them.

FLEXIBILITY

One summer, at Shoal Bay, as starting time for one of our beach mission services approached, conditions didn't look promising. Dark clouds were rolling in from the south-west and thunder rolled menacingly in the distance. Noticing that most of our anticipated audience had already gathered I signalled to the leader to make an early start.

Fearing that people would desert the service when the storm finally hit, I indicated to the team member who was to be the speaker that I wanted him to go straight on after the opening chorus. I hoped that the storm would be delayed long enough for him to give his message. As the sky grew darker and the thunder drew closer, he pressed on, valiantly ignoring the threatened downpour. Slowly the clouds rolled over us and the rumbles subsided without a single drop of rain falling. By the time the speaker had finished, the sun was shining, and all sign of the storm had passed.

Giving all the praise to the Lord we decided to carry on with all the other items that were a scheduled part of the meeting. The order of events was a complete reversal of what we had planned, but we were still able to include everything.

HELPING CHILDREN TO TRUST JESUS

It was Saturday morning when two boys knocked at the door of the house where I was staying in a country town.

'What is it fellas?' I asked. 'About what you said' they replied. I had told the children who attended the after-school clubs that they could come and see me any time if they wanted to know how to become Christians.

We found some seats in the back garden and I started to chat about Jesus. After a while I noticed that they seemed ill at ease. It must have taken lots of courage for them to seek me out and here I was being insensitive. I consciously let myself relax and casually asked a question about football. We talked about footy for a few minutes until I sensed that their nervousness had settled, then I led them back to the subject of trusting the Lord Jesus.

When we have opportunities for such significant conversations, we can be so anxious to do it well that we get tense. The children sense it and they too become nervous.

For such occasions, choose a location which is away from noise and activities, but not out of sight or secluded, as that might cause anxiety in the children and suspicion in their parents.

Begin by asking unthreatening questions that require a fuller answer than 'yes' or 'no'. 'What part of the talk to-day made you think of coming to see me?' 'Have you ever chatted with someone about how to trust Jesus?' 'What kind of things would you like us to do for you?' 'What is the thing you most think of when someone mentions Jesus?' 'What made you think of waiting to talk to me?' Open-ended questions like this help you find the clues to what the child is thinking.

Sometimes children worry a bit when they think they don't know the answers. I try to make light of it. 'I'm a silly duffer. I can see that question is confusing you. Let me try to say it another way.'

When we're helping children to take their first steps of conscious faith in the Lord Jesus, the following steps are essential.

1. We should help them see why they need to trust the Lord Jesus.
2. We should explain what the Lord Jesus has done for them—dying to forgive them and give them a new start, sending his Spirit to be with them always.
3. We should outline clearly what they can do to begin trusting the Lord Jesus. I suggest a 'sorry, thank you, please' prayer (see *Metaphors*).
4. We should show them how they can keep going with Jesus and growing their faith in him.

Booklets such as *Starting out* and *Trusting Jesus,* published by Scripture Union, are helpful.

HOLIDAY BIBLE CLUBS

How would you go about planning a Holiday Bible Club? The planning group must first think about questions such as these.

1. What will we call the activity? Holiday Club, Adventure Time, Kid's Klub, Orbit Inn, etc?
2. What will be its duration: 5 days, 10 days?
3. What will be the time slot? Two hours, 3 hours, all day?
4. Which age group will we cater for? Pre-school, infants, primaries, junior teens?
5. What activities will we include? Teaching, games, morning tea, craft, puppets?
6. How many helpers will we need?
7. Should we impose a charge for those who attend?
8. What avenues should we pursue in advertising? Leaflets, posters, banners, local papers, radio spots?
9. How many leaflets will we need and how will they be distributed? Through the schools, letterbox drop, etc?
10. Should we choose a theme on which to focus advertising, decorations, etc?

Once the major questions have been determined, the planning moves on to the day to day details with another batch of questions.

(a) How many sections will be formed? Who will lead them?
(b) What is the basic theme of our teaching?
(c) Which songs or choruses will reinforce this teaching?
(d) Who can we get to provide the music?
(e) Will the teaching be given by a leader or by team teaching or in individual class groups?
(f) Who will take charge of games?
(g) What will we give the children for morning tea?
(h) Who will organise the craft activities?
(i) Should there be a different craft project each day or something more difficult that will take the week to complete?
(j) Should we run a bus to collect the children?
(k) Should we take them home?
(l) Will we hold a function to conclude the week?
(m) What will this function be? A family night, a family barbecue or a luncheon on the final day?

This last question sets the group off on another round of questions that must be answered, e.g. What time will we hold it? Will we have a meal or only supper, and so on.

Having completed plans for the activity the group's work still isn't done. They must then ask themselves how they can capitalise on the contacts that are made with further follow-up contact and activities. While this may appear to be never ending it is far more effective in the long term than a series of one-off functions that have no conscious links with the rest of your group plans.

INVITING A RESPONSE

Good manuals on children's evangelism carry strong warnings about the way to invite children to respond to the good news of Jesus. Avoid demonstrative methods and don't encourage copy-cat responses, they say.

Some evangelists are happy to have an 'altar call' in children's meetings where the boys and girls are invited to come to the front of the meeting to show they wish to follow Jesus. Some invite children to raise their hands or stand up if they wish to 'belong to Jesus' or 'go to heaven'.

This has not been my approach and I would advise against the use of emotional pressure to enlist a response. We need to be sure that it is the Holy Spirit who is calling for the child's response and not human manipulation.

It is easy to warn people what not to do; what are some positive steps we can take to help children respond to Jesus? How do we link children who are genuinely open to Jesus with a sensitive, able and pastorally caring leader who can offer them the help they need?

My usual practice is to advise the whole group how they can trust the Lord Jesus. I outline a prayer of acceptance that they can pray at home. If you do this, it is essential to follow it up the next day by giving the children an opportunity for a personal chat either with yourself or other helpers. The invitation can be given along these lines.

'I know that some of you have been thinking very hard about the way the Lord Jesus can be your special friend and Saviour. Yesterday I suggested a prayer that you could pray at home. It was a 'sorry, thank you, please' prayer. Perhaps when you went home something happened and you were unable to do that. You could pray a prayer like that at home tonight if you want to trust Jesus and put him in first place in your life.

Some of you may have prayed that prayer last night. If you did I would like you to stay behind after we finish for a short time so that I can have a chat to you to make sure you understand what it all means.' [I usually explain that I intend finishing the meeting early to give time for this. In some instances where children are brought by bus or car you will need to explain that you have asked the drivers to wait, etc.]

Of course sometimes you may conduct a meeting that is not part of a series such as a mission; you will need to provide the children with an opportunity to make an immediate response. As you conclude the meeting you can say something like this.

'After we finish this meeting everyone will be going outside to play 'poison ball' with Jenny. While that happens I will be sitting over there (indicating location). If God has been speaking to you and you want to put your trust in the Lord Jesus you could come and talk to me about it.'

In this way you offer an alternative to the children so that they have a choice to make. The key is to avoid unnecessary emotional pressure while giving the children some definite course of action to follow.

When you have opportunities for personal conversation it is best to make it brief. Encourage your helpers to focus on the central issue to avoid over-loading the child with information. It is better to arrange several brief chats rather than trying to cover everything in one long and involved session. You can discuss topics like Bible reading, prayer and witness in a later conversation.

Try to have such chats in familiar surroundings where others can see what is going on. Parents may become concerned if they find that their children are meeting some unknown adult in private. Anyone who is aware of trends in today's community will understand parents' fears.

After dealing with the question of their relationship with the Lord, your next concern should be to establish a link between the child and some other Christian or a Christian fellowship that can nurture them until they become established in the faith.

Sometimes we are not in a position to arrange to hold personal chats with the children. In these instances I outline the prayer of commitment that the children can pray at home and I ask them to write a letter telling me what they have done. I explain that there will be a special letter box at the next meeting where they can 'post' their reply. Obviously this approach is not as helpful as face-to-face chat, yet I have discovered that often what the children write is very revealing.

In all of the above situations, it is helpful to give those who make some response some literature, e.g. the Scripture Union booklets *Starting out* or *Trusting Jesus*. Children can read these on their own, or you can work through them together. Never give the children any hints that you plan to hand out literature or you may find some who go through the process merely to get a free book.

(See also *Metaphors* and *Helping children to trust Jesus*).

JESUS

At a high school discussion group, a fourteen year old said, 'I believe in God and heaven and all that, it's the stories of Jesus that I find hard to accept!' 'I feel the same way', chimed in another in the group. 'These stories might all just be made up by somebody.'

This didn't surprise me, as I had heard similar statements on other occasions, but I was saddened to think that in some way our teaching about the Lord Jesus had an air of unreality about it. The teenagers' sentiments were echoed by an actress who was taking the part of a nun in a play, *Brides of Christ*. In a radio interview she described herself as a 'lapsed Catholic' and explained that she had begun to doubt such things as 'the infallibility of the Pope' and the 'virgin birth'.

I was disturbed to hear these concepts bracketed together, yet

I have to agree that, at first sight, such stories as the virgin birth, and Jesus turning water into wine and raising the dead seem unreal. On reflection, it is obvious that if the gospel writers had merely invented stories which they wanted to dress up as fact, they would not have included the miracles. Instead they claim to have been eye-witnesses of the events that they recorded and our faith is based on our assessment of their reliability as witnesses. To help children build an understanding of Jesus as a historical person, four tips come to mind.

1. Give attention to detail

Watch for the simple details that give incidents from the Gospels the ring of reality and include them in your presentation.

For example, when the conversation between the Lord Jesus and the woman of Samaria was abruptly interrupted by the return of the disciples (John 14:27), she 'left her water jar' and hurried back to the city to tell others about Jesus. Obviously it would be difficult to hurry carrying a water jar but otherwise this statement appears to have no other significance. The mention of the woman leaving her water pot behind gives the account the stamp of authenticity.

On some occasions one of the Gospel writers will give some detail that all the others miss. Examining all of the accounts of an event gives the fullest possible picture and enables you to discover details you would miss if reading the story in only one Gospel. For example, if we compare the accounts of the feeding of the five thousand we find the following differences.
- Mark is the only one to report that the grass was green.
- John is the only one to mention the boy with the loaves and fishes.
- John is also the only one to tell us of Philip's protest that 'eight months' wages' would be needed to purchase food for such a large crowd.

2. Show that Jesus was special

John sums up Jesus' character in the phrase, 'full of grace and truth' (1:14), and we must be careful always to depict him in ways that are true to this statement. In my experience one truth that has been successfully communicated to the children in our churches is that the Lord Jesus was sinless. This is not as a result of any formal lesson on the subject, but is a cumulative understanding that they have acquired. Ask any class of children whether Jesus would ever lie or cheat or break a promise and their answer indicates that this is unthinkable.

It is quite stunning to realise that of all the characters of literature both real and fictitious, only the Lord Jesus is described as morally perfect. No other person has ever faced his critics with the challenge 'Can any of you prove me guilty of sin?' John 8:46—and no-one could.

3. Report Jesus' emotions

'Jesus wept', (John 11:35) is, as you probably know, the shortest verse in the Bible. More importantly it helps us recognise that Jesus was truly human. The Gospels record many occasions when he was moved by compassion when confronted with human suffering and need.

On other occasions we see:
- his tenderness as he reassures Mary in the garden
- his firmness as he drives the traders from the temple
- his amazement at the centurion's faith
- his distress because of the hard-heartedness of those who criticised him for healing on the Sabbath.

4. Mention the reactions of those who met Jesus

As we describe the way Jesus' friends and enemies reacted to him, it helps the children realise that these were real people responding to events that actually took place.

I can imagine Philip gabbling excitedly as he approached his friend, Nathanael.

'We have found the one Moses wrote about in the Law and about whom the prophets also wrote. Jesus of Nazareth, the son of Joseph' (John 1:45).

Can't you hear the disdain in Nathanael's voice as he sneeringly replies: 'Nazareth! Can anything good come from there?' His tone soon changes as he overhears Jesus' remark about him and asks: 'How do you know me?' His tone would change yet again as he declares: 'Rabbi, you are the Son of God, you are the King of Israel.'

When studying an incident such as this, take careful note of the changing emotions. Try to express them in your tone of voice when you tell the story.

Another example of emotional responses worth noting is Luke's account of the resurrection. Have you noticed that the disciples did not believe the news that the grave of Jesus was empty? 'What the women told them seemed to them like nonsense' (Luke 24:11).

It is important for our pupils to realise that even those who were involved were sceptical until they were confronted by overwhelming evidence of the presence of the risen Christ. Thomas is the prime example of this (John 20:25).

(See also *Embellishment*)

LANGUAGE BARRIERS

I had invited Kyoshi Iwai, a visiting Japanese colleague, to tea. Knowing that my wife was ill in bed I thought it best to prepare my guest for the situation at home.

'I'm afraid', I said, 'We'll have to take pot luck tonight as I'm chief cook and bottle washer at present.'

A puzzled look came over Kyoshi's face.

'Chief cook and bottle-washer, what is this?' he asked in bewilderment. I had forgotten that while my guest was fluent in English he had not been initiated into the intricacies of Australian slang.

Similarly, in communicating the Christian faith it is easy to confuse people by using language that is only intelligible to the initiated. Through growing up outside of Christian influences in my childhood, I believe I have been more sensitive than most to this problem.

One of the areas where this problem becomes most apparent is in our use of hymns and choruses. Unfortunately, this sort of thing happens all the time. For example, on the first night of a beach mission, the marquee was crowded with campers, both children and adults who had been rounded up by the team.

'Let's sing, "Great is the Lord", announced the enthusiastic young leader. The musicians struck up the tune and the campers sang with gusto.

Beautiful for situation, the joy of the whole earth,
Is Mount Zion on the sides of the north,
   the city of the great King.

The singing was loud enough for the leader to be unaware that the uninitiated, of whom there were plenty, did not participate. How could they? Despite a pleasant tune, the words are mumbo jumbo to anyone not in the inner circle. The younger the group, the greater this difficulty becomes. I have often observed that very small children sing sounds that are like the words when the lyrics are beyond their understanding.

Another area of ministry where 'the language of Zion' is frequently used is in public prayer. 'We pray that you will undertake for Joe, etc.' The uninitiated could be forgiven for assuming we were expecting Joe to die, as that is the time we normally call for the undertaker.

The trouble is that we become more experienced in using and understanding Christian jargon with the passage of time. It is easy to lose sight of the fact that what we are saying may mean something entirely different to others, especially children.

Sometimes the problem may be an experience barrier rather than a language barrier. At a family barbecue the organisers were delighted at the roll-up of outsiders. Many of the people present, I was told, 'never darken the door of a church'. After the meal when we gathered together for the meeting, the pastor's wife led some chorus singing. 'Let's start with, "It's no longer I that liveth, but Christ that liveth in me," ' she announced enthusiastically. The words of this chorus aren't difficult, but they are inappropriate words to ask a group of unbelievers to sing.

LINKS IN STORYTELLING

A good talk has a natural flow from one point to the next. By placing things in their proper order you will avoid having to say, 'I meant to tell you such and such', and you will retain the attention and confidence of your audience.

Finding some item that serves as a connecting link can assist cohesion. The talk outline below tells the story of the healing of the paralysed man from Mark 2 using the man's bed (or mat) as the flow-through link.

Talk outline

[As an introduction discuss how uncomfortable a bed becomes if you are ill. This gives you a way in to talk about the paralysed man.] There was a man in Capernaum who could never get out of bed because he was paralysed. His bed was like a prison, he could never leave it.

[Recount what his friends told him about the visit of the Lord Jesus.] It must have been very painful to be carried through that crowd and worse still as they struggled to carry his bed up onto the roof of the house. The worst was still to come. Lying on his mat, the man must have been terrified as he dangled through that hole in the roof, hoping the crowd would make enough space on the floor for him to land. When finally the mat hit the floor boards with a bone-jarring thump he must have wondered whether it was all worth it.

Looking up from his mat he could see the faces of his friends peering through the ceiling. Everyone in the crowd was staring at him. Some looked surprised, others looked annoyed. What would Jesus do?

'Son, your sins are forgiven!'

[Explain what sin is and remind the group that sin prevents us from living in a way that pleases God. Then explain that the paralysed man had allowed himself to be lowered into that crowded room confidently expecting that the Lord Jesus could cure his paralysis.] He got much more than he expected—the forgiveness of his sins. When I ask the Lord Jesus to forgive my sin I can confidently expect that he will.

To prove to the people who were present especially the teachers of the law who were critical of him, that he had the power to forgive sin, Jesus spoke to the man again. He ordered him to pick up his mat and go home. They were all astonished when he pushed his way out through the crowd with his mat tucked under his arm.

That night when the man went to bed he must have looked at that mat and thought to himself, 'This mat is no longer my prison. I needn't be frightened of lying down. When I wake up in the morning I'll be able to get up and go wherever I want to.'

LOST AND FOUND

Being lost is one way the Gospels describe what it's like to be out of touch with God. In shorthand, we are lost because our sinfulness keeps us away from God. Being 'lost' doesn't mean that we are forgotten or lost by God as if he can't figure out a way to reach us. It is simply that we've walked away. Either we've done this deliberately or else we've never bothered to accept his welcome to belong to his family.

The ever-popular story of Zacchaeus is a good illustration of this idea. The problem is that some children know this enchanting story very well. So this outline depends for its method on a question and answer approach, which can be supplemented with simple sketches if you wish.

Talk outline

Have you ever been lost? [Discuss with the group what it is like to be lost. A good example would be becoming separated from parents at the Easter show, and being taken to the lost children's tent.]

My story is about a little man who was lost [commence sketch].

It wasn't that he didn't know where he was, but Jesus said that this man was lost. Let's see if we can work out why. When Jesus visited Jericho, Zacchaeus wanted to see him but he was too short to see over the heads of the people in the crowd. What did he do? [Sketch in two eyes peering through the branches. Answer: He climbed a tree]

When Jesus came past he told Zacchaeus to come down. What did Jesus say he wanted to do? [Go home for a meal]

Many of the people in the crowd were annoyed. 'Listen to that! He's going to be the guest of a man who is a . . .?' [After giving the children time to guess at what the people may have said, give them the answer—A sinner. Discuss the question—what is a sinner? Explain that sin is both doing wrong and also not doing what is right, giving an example of each of these aspects of sin.] In what way was Zacchaeus a sinner? [Usually they identify that he was a cheat.] If sin is also not doing right, what was it that Zacchaeus had failed to do? [Your audience are unlikely to answer readily and may need the following clues.]

Besides repaying anyone he had cheated what did Zacchaeus promise to do? 'Give half of his goods to the poor'. There had always been lots of poor people in Jericho but until he met Jesus Zacchaeus hadn't bothered about them. What are some of the things *we* have failed to do? Zacchaeus had only been interested in himself. He had been ignoring God and his ways. This is what Jesus meant when he said that Zacchaeus was 'lost'. When Zacchaeus promised to give half of his possessions to the poor and to repay any he had cheated with four times the amount, Jesus announced 'Salvation has come to this man's house.' [It will probably be necessary to explain the word salvation—if I fall overboard out of a boat and someone rescues me, I have been saved from drowning.]

Who was Zacchaeus saved from? [Himself!] He was rescued from being lost. Even someone that everybody hated, like Zacchaeus, was valuable to the Lord Jesus.

LOVE

Children today are brainwashed through the television, cinema, videos and popular music with a Hollywood version of love. This outline, based on an exciting Old Testament story, should help them understand what true love is.

Talk outline

Do you know what love is? Is it falling in love when you meet someone who is very attractive? [Amplify with humour]

In fact, love is more than that. Let me give you an example.

It's your mother's birthday and you go to the shop and buy her a present. [When I was a child I bought my mother some Cashmere Bouquet soap every birthday—you may have a similar example you can give.]

When you give your mum her present she seems so pleased and gives you a big hug because she loves you. Later on that day when your mother asks you to do something for her, you whinge and refuse.

'I'm too busy!' you grumble or 'Why can't Jenny do it?' (After all what are sisters for?).

If I am obedient and helpful I prove by my actions that I really do love my mother. Let me tell you one of the greatest love stories of history to help you understand what love is.

[Introduce David, Bethlehem, the Philistine soldiers—2 Samuel 23. Sketch a Palestinian scene.]

At the time of our story David, who was now a King, and his men had been beaten and the Philistines had captured Beth-lehem. David and his soldiers were forced to hide in caves up in the hills. Poor David! He felt really miserable.

'If only someone could bring me a drink of water from the well that is near the gate at Bethlehem' he muttered.

Some of David's men looked at each other and quietly slipped away.

'Our King wants a drink of water from Bethlehem!'

'Then we should get it for him shouldn't we?'

'What about the Philistines?'

'We're not going to let a few Philistines stop us are we?'

'No, I suppose not. All right, I'll get a wineskin to carry the water'.

These men loved David so much that they would risk anything to please him. They made their plans and the three of them set off across the hills towards Bethlehem.

'Wow! Look at them! They're everywhere.' [Sketch in extras.]

'Right. When we get to the well, we'll hold them off while you get the water. Are you ready? Let's. . .GO!' [Sketch in the first man running towards the well.]

'Tanta ran ta ta!' The bugles of the watchmen on the walls started blaring.

Philistine soldiers rushed to man the walls. [Sketch them in.]

'Hurry men! The Israelites are attacking.' [Sketch in second runner.]

'But. . .there's only three of them. Come on, let's attack.'

They opened the great gate and the Philistines poured out like ants. [Sketch them in.] Soon the charging Israelites found their way barred by the leading Philistines, but they fought their way through so fiercely that the Philistines fell back. [Sketch in third man behind the well.]

'Keep them back while I get the water.'

'OK. I've got enough. Fall back.'

They fought their way back and the Philistines let them go. [Describe the men limping back to their camp.]

'Pass the word, someone's coming!'

'Say, its some of our blokes.'

'What's happened?'

Without bothering to reply, the three warriors pushed their way through into the cave where King David was. They knelt down [suit your actions to your words] and offered the king a cup of water.

'Wha–wha–what's this?' stammered David.

'Water, your majesty. Water from the well at Bethlehem!'

'From wh. . .wh–where? Bethlehem!. But, but. . .'

As David took that cup his hand trembled. He was a warrior himself and he had a good idea of what they had been through. In that moment he knew what love really was.

'I. . .I can't drink this! This water is too precious. This is like the blood of these faithful men. God is the only one who is worthy of a gift of this value. I'm going to pour it out as a way of worshipping God!'

David took that precious water and poured it out as an offering to the Lord.

Sometimes, when we really think about how loving God is to us, we wonder how we can show him that we love him too. Let me tell you what one person did about this. In Europe a couple of centuries ago lived a wealthy young man called Count Zinzendorf who went to an art gallery one day to see an art exhibition. [Sketch the scene.]

One picture in particular caught his eye—it showed the Lord Jesus hanging on the cross. Underneath the picture the young man read these words: 'All this I did for you, what have you done for me?'

He read the words over and over again. 'All this I did for you, what have you done for me?'

Count Zinzendorf realised in that moment just how great God's love was. He left the art gallery a different person. Up till then he thought only of himself, now he wanted to do what he could to help people hear about the love of the Lord Jesus.

With his money he founded the Moravian Missionary Society that sent people to many parts of the world to preach the Christian message. If you say you love God, what can you do to show it? The hardest thing is to live our lives the way we know he wants us to. Jesus said 'If you love me, keep my commandments.'

[Footnote: Depending on your group you may feel you need to add that our salvation does not depend upon the things we do. We demonstrate our faith by what we do. Be careful not to finish with a long and complicated conclusion.]

MEMORISING BIBLE VERSES

A Bible College student reminded me that he had attended a mission I conducted when he was a schoolboy.

'I can still remember the verse you taught us.' To prove it he repeated the verse perfectly. 'I think that was the first verse I ever really learned' he said. 'I was so eager to get the prize at the end of the week that I prayed about it and God helped me learn it.'

Obviously the experience was very important to him.

When teaching children to memorise Scripture, aim to teach it so thoroughly that they will be able to recall it, perhaps for the rest of their lives. If they can repeat a verse this week but stumble over it a fortnight later, they have not really learned it.

Your teaching has not been thorough enough. Your objective should be that the larger proportion of the children will know it, not merely the brighter ones.

The key to success is constant repetition. While there are many useful ideas to make memory work fun such as puzzle texts, mystery letterings, etc, many people make the mistake of spending too much time on puzzles and insufficient time getting the children to repeat the words. It is important to have the words of the verse up before them fairly quickly and then to spend more time on repetition.

A technique that I have found particularly effective is to focus on a long verse or a short passage and teach a short segment of it each day. The key to this method is to begin at the start of the verse each time you repeat it.

If you recognise that God's word committed to memory can be of great benefit to those who learn it, you will choose the verses with great care, making sure that they will be of greatest blessing. Verses from the Bible well remembered and understood can be a great help, often many years later.

It is worth noting five questions when selecting Bible passages for memory work.

1. Does the section stand well alone or have you distorted its message by taking it out of its context in the Bible?
2. Have you chosen a simple translation that makes sense to the children?
3. Are there any difficult words or ideas that should be explained?
4. How will you help the children to discover the application of the Bible truth in their lives?
5. Have your methods detracted from the significance and authority of this part of the Word of God?

METAPHORS

Increasingly in my own ministry I have become aware of the difficulties children have in dealing with metaphorical and figurative language. We do well to avoid it when we can.

A mother was speaking to her 8 year old daughter about asking Jesus to 'come into her heart'. Her four year old, who was listening to the conversation, interrupted with a serious question: 'What happens to Jesus when the food goes down?'

We chuckle when we hear of these quaint misunderstandings but often we are not prepared to admit that children have a problem when confronted with figurative language.

In helping children to faith, for example, I encourage them to use three straightforward ideas in a prayer—sorry, thank you and please. 'I'm sorry for my sin. Thank you for dying on the cross for me. Please forgive me and be my Saviour!' I am well aware that in avoiding figurative language, I have run into another problem: theological concepts such as sin and saviour. These are not everyday words, and their meaning can be difficult to grasp. Take care to explain them in your teaching sessions in a way that children will understand. After all, these theological terms occur frequently in the Bible. If we wish to encourage children to read the Bible, we must be ready to teach them what these words mean.

NAMES

At any camp I lead, my goal is to be able to address each camper by name by the end of the second day of camp. This may mean that I ask some children a number of times before being able to commit their names to memory. On one occasion a boy was overheard to say, 'Isn't it beaut! Commy knows my name now.' I must have asked him three of four times before it registered. Knowing a person's name is the first step in establishing a relationship.

In areas where there is a high ethnic population some names may be unfamiliar to us and we must make the effort to learn these names correctly. It may seem funny to us if we think their name is unpronounceable—but it isn't to them. Similarly we must be careful not to make fun of a child's name. It is tempting to make a joke if a boy is called 'Angel' or 'Hercules' but don't or you may hurt his feelings.

One technique that I have used at the commencement of a series of meetings is to have an OHP transparency with an illustration of some kind and the word 'welcome' on it. I ask the children to put up their hands if their name starts with the letter A and as I ask them their names I write them up. After about ten or a dozen I pause and say 'let me see if I can remember who belongs to these names.' I then point out each one in turn. This is a great help in getting to know the children's names.

At any one session don't attempt to record too many names. In a large group choose a few letters at random each day.

OBEYING GOD'S WORD

The main purpose of this talk outline is to encourage obedience to what God says. It uses an imaginary character who is similar to many who would have been alive at the time of Josiah's reform (2 Kings 22). The dialogue is given in full as an example of how this kind of biblical story can be brought to life. Notice that the details suggested in the outline are in harmony with the biblical account; no liberty is taken that is outside the realm of historical accuracy (see *Embellishment*). The outline has a sketch-talk format and uses the sketching method explained in the section *Quick sketching*.

Talk outline

[Turn to a picture of a large tree.]

Chop! Chop! Chop! The sound of chopping echoed through the forest. [Sketch in the axeman.]

'Hi, what are you doing?' [Sketch in second man.]

'I'm chopping down a tree!'

'I can see that! What are you going to do with it?'

'I'm going to carve an Asherah pole!'

'An Asherah pole! But this tree's too big! It'll take you months to carve a goddess that size!'

'I suppose it will, but it'll be worth it. I reckon the bigger the carving the more powerful it must be.'

'I suppose you're right. Let me know when you finish and I'll help you drag it out of the forest.'

'Thanks, I'll need all the help I can get!'

While this man is imaginary, there were many like him back when the people of Israel had neglected the worship of the one true God and had begun to worship the gods of some of the other people in nearby countries. Asherah was the name of a goddess who was supposed to be the wife of Baal.

'Chop, chop, chop!' The chopping went on day after day for weeks until finally—'Crack!' Down crashed the forest giant.

[For your second picture sketch in the man chipping at the log with a hammer and chisel.]

'Chip, chip, chip!'

'This is going to take you forever,' said the man's wife. [Sketch her in.] 'Why did you pick on such a big tree?'

'Well, I've prayed to the other Asherah poles but they don't answer my prayers. I thought if I made a bigger one it would be more powerful.'

'What about the work you need to do on the house. The roof leaks and the door has sagged and the window. . .'

'It'll have to wait. I want to finish this new goddess first!'

His wife was about to complain again when she noticed something very interesting. As he worked, a little pile of chips was building up under the log. With winter coming she was going to have plenty of chips for the stove. [Sketch in heap of chips.]

When the pole was finally finished, all the neighbours agreed it was the best goddess they had ever seen and certainly the biggest. It was erected near the temple in Jerusalem, and lots of people came to worship it including King Amon. [Sketch in people bowing before the idol.]

The artist was very pleased. It made him feel very important that the king himself had come to worship the idol he had made [Sketch in the king.]

His wife was very pleased. There was a huge pile of chips, enough to keep the stove going for months.

Kerlop, kerlop, kerlop. The hoofbeats of the messenger's horse rattled along the stony road.

'The king is dead!' he shouted. 'Long live the King.'

'What's happened? The king was only a young man. How could he be dead so soon?'

'Some of his officials sneaked into his palace and killed him. Josiah his son has taken his place.'

'Josiah! He's only a boy!'

'That's right! He's eight years of age!'

How would you like to be king at the age of eight? Sounds like fun, doesn't it. Of course his mother was able to help him until he was older but even though he was only eight he was wiser than his father had been. 'He did what was right in the eyes of the Lord.' (2 Kings 22:3). [Describe Josiah visiting the temple and discovering the state of its disrepair and recount the orders he gave for its restoration—2 Kings 22:3-7.]

While they were busy at work Hilkiah the priest made a wonderful discovery. 22:8. He found the Book of the Law (this was part of the Bible).

'Shaphan! Come quickly! Look what I've found!'

'What is it Hilkiah?'

'The Book of the Law!'

'Here! Let me see it. This has been missing for years, I must show the King.'

'The Book of the Law!' said King Josiah. 'Isn't that the book that records the laws the Lord God gave to Moses? Read it to me.'

Shaphan unrolled the scroll and started to read.

' "I am the Lord your God, who brought you out of Egypt, out of the land of slavery. You shall have no other gods before me" ' (Deuteronomy 5:6).

'What, no other gods! What about Baal and Molech and Asherah?'

'I'm sure it means that we shouldn't worship those gods. Listen, "You shall not make for yourself an idol in the form of anything in heaven above or on the earth beneath or in the waters below." '

'But the country's full of idols. The Lord must be very angry with us. Quickly, find out for me what our disobedience will mean.'

Many people live their lives in ignorance of what the Bible says. It is only when we take time to read it for ourselves that we discover God's plan for our lives.

[Recount the visit of Hilkiah and Shaphan to Huldah the prophetess and report the message of encouragement she sent to the king.] When Josiah received Huldah's message he knew it was time for a change. When we take time to find out what God wants of us it will bring a change in our lives too.

The Bible gives us very clear instruction about the way God wants us to behave. Listen to this verse [it is sometimes a good idea to actually read out from a Bible rather than simply quoting]. 'Do not lie to each other.' If boys or girls trust in the Lord Jesus do you think they can continue to tell lies whenever they feel like it? Of course not! God wants us to turn away from those things we know are wrong to live his way instead.

Tan ta ta ra ta ta! The trumpet call rang out throughout the city square. The people who had gathered grew quiet.

'Listen everybody! The book of the law has been found and his majesty the King has ordered me to read it to you. "This is what the Lord God says, 'You shall not make for yourself an idol in the form of anything in heaven above or on the earth beneath or in the waters below. You shall not bow down to them or worship them for I the Lord your God am a jealous God!' " '

As the words rang out, the people looked at one another.

'What does this mean?'

'Probably means we should scrap all our idols!'

'But what about my Asherah Pole? I carved it all myself. It took me months of work!'

'Sounds like it'll have to be smashed!'

'What! They can't! They wouldn't dare!'

'Sssh. Listen! The King is speaking.'

'My people! You have heard what the Lord God has said. Now you must follow the Lord and do the things he commands us. All false gods and idols will have to go. We will worship only him'.

'Yes!' shouted the people. 'We will worship only him. Away with these useless idols.'

'Someone get an axe! Start on that Asherah Pole.'

It wasn't long before the pole was smashed and blazing

merrily on a huge bonfire. [Turn to fourth picture].

When we study the Bible, it will have an effect on our lives too. Remember what I said about not telling lies? That's just one example.

'My Asherah,' wailed the artist. 'Look what they've done to my Asherah! All that work wasted!'

'Never mind dear,' said his wife. 'I still have a lovely heap of chips at home.'

OLDER CHILDREN

In any situation where there is a wide age range, you must always be aware of the different attitudes of the older children. Visiting a country Sunday school I noticed that the older children i.e. the 12 to 14 year olds, were irritated by the program and that the leader was unaware of the problem.

'Come on you big ones at the back. You're not doing the actions!'

They scowled at him and reluctantly moved their arms to sing 'Wide, wide as the ocean'. I later persuaded the coordinator to form a separate department for these children to keep them from activities that were beneath their dignity.

When conducting an after school mission I prefer to limit the age group to say 8's to 12's. The reason for this is not that the younger children are difficult but that the older children stay away if the session is swamped with babies. A program that is tailored to the older primaries can be greeted with, 'This is just for the little kids!', if the younger group is predominant.

Keep this in mind if you are starting kid's clubs or similar activities.

OVERHEAD PROJECTORS

The overhead projector is a tool I use constantly. While they are readily available, few people use them to their fullest potential; many spoil their presentation by making lettering and pictures too small.

When using the OHP, always follow these rules.

1. Maximise the letter size

Make 36 point, the equivalent of half an inch (12.5 mm), your minimum size and you can't go wrong.

2. Minimise the content

Do not try to cram too much material on to each transparency. OHP books recommend a limit of six to eight words per line and six to eight lines per visual. While this may be too limiting, if you are projecting the words of choruses or hymns it is a good guideline to go by. For example *never* cram two choruses onto one transparency. If the chorus is a short one make the lettering larger and spread it out.

3. Enliven with colour

While it is best to print in black, especially if you intend to use the material in daylight, you can use colour in a variety of ways to give your presentation a lift. Pictures can be coloured in with overhead projector pens. This greatly enhances your presentation. Use permanent pens, not those labelled 'temporary', as these will smudge with use.

You can also add colour with what is termed 'colour adhesive film' or by using 'billboarding film'. Ask your OHP supplier for details of these products.

4. Create interest with pictures

The best way to produce a transparency is with a plain paper copier using the special transparencies that have been developed for this purpose. All you do is place your master under the lid and the transparency in the paper feed and press the button. You can add illustrations clipped from various sources to your 'master sheet' before you copy it. Words of hymns or choruses are much more interesting if accompanied with a colourful illustration.

The overhead projector has other uses as well. You can use it to inject novelty into the teaching of memory texts. Overleaf is a sample based on Luke 15:3–7.

To make a transparency from the illustration, first enlarge it to fill an A4 sheet of paper. For your transparency frame, take a piece of cardboard and cut out of it an octagonal shape of the same size as the enlarged illustration.

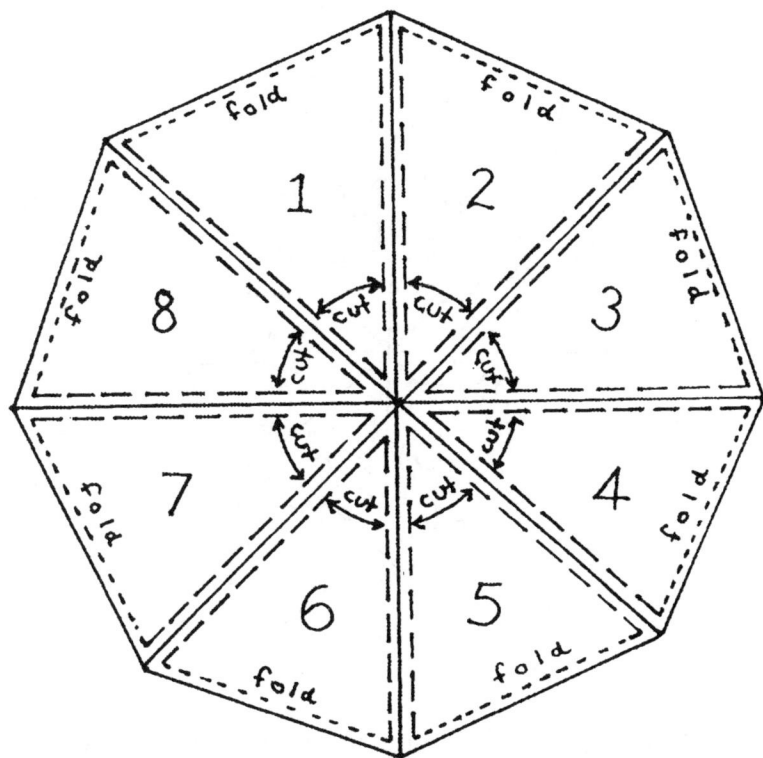

As shown above, use the cardboard octagon to make eight triangular cover flaps. Cut along the broken lines, leaving a few millimetres at the outside edge so that the flaps remain attached. Number the flaps as shown and attach them above the transparency. As you teach the memory verses, fold back each of the flaps in turn to reveal the illustrations.

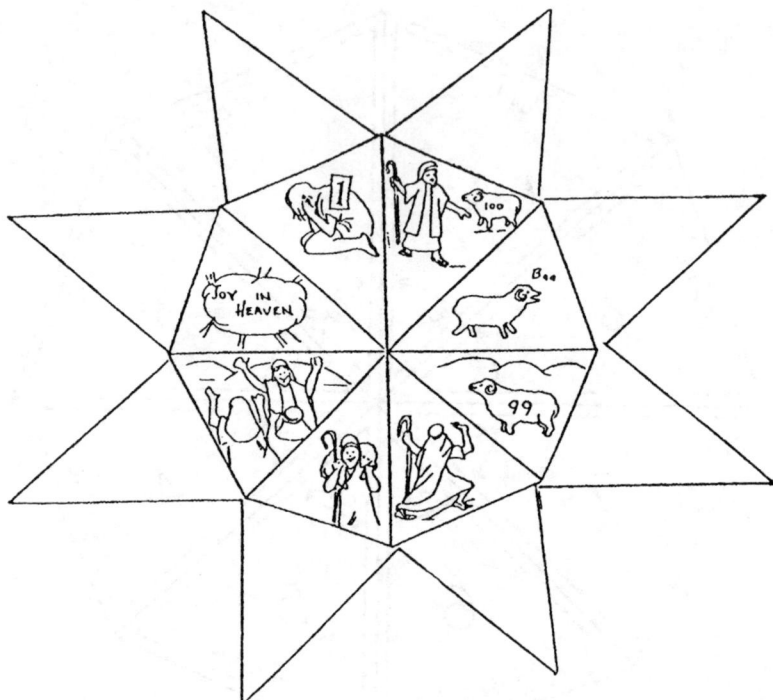

Above is shown the illustration with the cover flaps attached and folded out.

You can also project silhouette figures or art-work overlays to tell a Bible story. My book *Visualised Bible stories for the overhead projector*, available from Christian bookshops, uses cardboard cut outs to form silhouetted pictures similar to those in a shadow puppet play. It is also possible to project art figures and tell the story in a similar way to using a flan-o-graph. Overhead projector stories of this type can be described as 'Flan-o-graph with a modern face'. My book *Joseph visualised for the overhead projector* contains the stories of Joseph's life prepared for use in this way.

(See *Visual aids, Visi-wheel story*)

PARTICIPATION

Children like participating. Wherever possible, involve them in what you do. The simplest form of involvement is to help. For example, many children are familiar with the overhead projector and can change over transparencies for you. Even those who express confidence should be shown how to handle the material properly so that they don't put the transparency on upside down or on a slant. Many fail to understand that if the plate is square with the light field of the projector it will be positioned correctly on the screen, assuming that the projector has been lined up beforehand.

Children enjoy being chosen to be captains. If you run an overhead projector quiz game, you can choose two captains who move the markers on the screen representing their team. If the team wins the quiz, then the 'captain' gets a reward of some kind. Buzzer or bell quiz competitions are also popular.

Visualised memory texts give the children an opportunity to come to the front to hold things or participate in other ways. You can chose children to hold up song cards or to lead the actions for an action song; you can also select children to respond in a conversation with a puppet or a ventriloquial doll. Older children could help as puppeteers, provided there is time available for them to practice with you beforehand.

While most children enjoy participating, some become self conscious when out in front and as a result, they can become a hindrance rather than a help, e.g. a boy who deliberately holds up a card upside down. In such an instance I would act calmly and decisively, either taking the card away and either signalling the child to return to his place without comment, or saying, 'I'm sorry, but I don't think you can be sensible enough today, perhaps I'll pick you again tomorrow.'

Never resort to ridicule or show your irritation by making a cutting remark; such actions only serve to put a barrier between you and the child concerned. If you find it necessary to correct a child in the group, find an opportunity to relate positively to him at a later point in time so that it is clear that you don't bear any animosity. It is wisest not to refer back to the incident as this may give the impression that you are apologising for being firm.

PLANNING

'Orbit Inn' was the delightful name of an after school club. The leaders invited me to visit them and give advice on improving their program. I think I learned more from them than I was able to contribute. The way they gave thorough attention to planning impressed me. When I asked what it was that they hoped I could contribute, their reply was, 'We have been running the club for two terms and we are running out of ideas!' How many children's clubs and Sunday schools do you know that carry on year in and year out totally unaware that their program is in a rut?

This group only functioned during school term time. 'We use the holidays to prepare for the next term!' They certainly had the right idea. Many of us are guilty of trying to run things 'by the seat of the pants' and wonder why our program fails to appeal. Whatever the activity—beach mission, holiday club, after school club or Sunday school, thoughtful planning and thorough preparation are essential for successful ministry.

The first task is to determine your target group. Will the activity be open to all children or only those connected with your church? Is the family camp designed to reach families 'on the fringe' or only those who are actively involved in the church? Once you have answered these questions you should go all out to contact and attract people who fit these guidelines.

The best Sunday school I have ever observed was led by a man who left nothing to chance. For example he recorded in a notebook the name of the teacher he had asked to be responsible for the offertory the following week. At the appropriate moment he would announce 'We will now have our offertory,' and the appointed teacher would come forward with two children whom he had chosen for the privilege. The teacher passed the plates to these children who took them round the group. On completion of their round they returned to the front where their teacher led the dedicatory prayer and the three then returned to their places. The contrast between this and the way it is normally done in most Sunday schools was most marked.

PRAYERS

Prayer is not a ritual that must be performed at the commencement and the conclusion of every meeting; this idea is a spill over from the adult church service. Many a time I have observed the leader of a meeting struggling to gain control to lead a closing prayer. 'We're going to stay here until you are quiet', the leader thunders. After a series of threats, the children are quiet and the leader manages to mumble a prayer, usually one in which the children have no interest or sense of participation.

In preference to ranting at the children to be quiet so that you can pray, it may be best to do your praying privately.

Alternatively you could ask the children to repeat phrases of a prayer after you. This is an acceptable practice with younger children, but I have observed that older primary age children generally do not react positively to this approach. If you use responsive prayer of this type you need to prepare what you intend to say beforehand, perhaps even write it out. That way, you will avoid falling into the trap of the unprepared leader whose prayer often begins with short phrases that become longer and more complex as it progresses.

Some other cautions to remember when engaging in public prayer are—be brief; don't preach a sermon; don't use a special voice or a special language. What could 'Oh Lord, we pray that you will undertake for us' mean to a child?

PROPITIATION

Now there's a word you wouldn't try to use with children! Most adults don't understand it either. James Packer, however, states in his book *Knowing God* that propitiation is at the heart of the gospel. If this is true then the concept, though not the word itself, must be part of our teaching if we are to share the gospel fully.

To define the term, propitiation is 'the appeasement of wrath through the offer of a gift'. In Christian theology, Jesus is seen as the propitiation for our sinfulness (1 John 4:10). When you think it through, in Jesus' death we see God paying his own price to satisfy his own sense of justice. When speaking to children about God and his anger against sin, we must be careful to keep the balance and not overstate the point. Our God 'delights' in mercy and it was because of his great love for us while we were still sinners that Christ died for us (Romans 5:8). Consider the following.

Talk outline

An episode of the TV program 'The World Around Us' featured the volcanoes of Hawaii. The film showed a group of experts in their protective clothing checking to see when the volcano was likely to erupt. [Sketch a volcano.]

DRAW
LAVA
IN RED

The film also showed some of the islanders throwing fruit and vegetables into the bubbling lava. [Sketch them in.] In would go a huge bunch of bananas or a box full of paw-paws and the people would rush down to get some more. These people were frantic.

The narrator explained the reason for their strange behaviour. The people from that village believe the volcano is a god. As it was threatening to erupt, they must have done something to make their god angry. They were throwing fruit and vegetables into the mountain to show that they were sorry. Their hope was that the volcano wouldn't be angry any more and would calm down.

What they were doing was quite useless however, because the volcano was only a volcano and not a god at all. God isn't part of his own creation. But the idea they had wasn't entirely foolish. God is terribly disappointed with our selfishness and dishonesty and cruelty and everything else about us that is sinful. In fact you could say he hates it.

Giving a gift to turn away anger isn't silly either. When David went out to face Goliath the giant in single handed combat, and beat him, he was everybody's favourite. People were dancing and singing in the street. 'Saul (their King) has slain his thousands and David his tens of thousands.'

Of course Saul hadn't slain thousands and David had only defeated one. What they meant was that King Saul was a great warrior but David was much much greater. This made King Saul very jealous and he asked David to come to play the harp for him. As David played, the king picked up a javelin and 'Zap' he threw it at David—but it missed.

David ran for his life and for the next few years lived as an outlaw out in the hills while King Saul's soldiers tried to capture him. David's family joined him there as well as anybody else who was in trouble or couldn't pay his debts or had deserted from the army (1 Samuel 22:1).

[Draw three blank faces on the board and as you do recount the story of David requesting food from Nabal (1 Samuel 25:1-11).]

When David heard of Nabal's refusal, he looked like this [sketch in anger lines].

'Right men, put on your swords!' thundered David. 'Two hundred of you stay here with our belongings, the rest of you come with me. We'll fix this Nabal, the ungrateful wretch!' We too have neglected to give God what he deserves. This is called sin and it makes God very angry.

[Describe Abigail's reaction when she was told about the threatened attack (1 Samuel 25:14-17).] Abigail didn't waste any time. Ordering her servants to bring a string of donkeys with gifts (1 Samuel 25:18), she headed for the hills to meet David. They met in a narrow gully and when David saw the loaded donkeys, his mouth dropped open and he stared in amazement [sketch in this expression on the second face].

[Recount the argument that Abigail used to persuade David as she points out that his intended action would be a stain on his reputation, 25:30-31.] As Abigail informed David of the items included in her gift, his expression changed. [Sketch in smiling expression on the third face.]

David accepted Abigail's gift and turned back to his camp peacefully. [Briefly complete the story with reference to Nabal's death and David's marriage proposal to Abigail. A woman of character like this was too good to miss.]

God loves us very, very much but he hates the evil in our lives—the things like cheating, lying, envy, spitefulness and greed. What can we offer to God to ask him not to be angry any more?

[Children will give a variety of answers and you must deal with each one as it is given, pointing out that loving God, or praying or going to church or even giving him our lives, cannot adequately pay for our failures.]

Our lives have been spoiled by sin and so we can never be good enough to pay for our failure to live God's way. Because God knew this he gave the gift himself (John 3:16). Jesus took the punishment of our sin upon himself. [Sketch in the cross.]

PUPPETS

An after school club asked for my help with their club's break-up. I agreed to perform a puppet version of *The lion, the witch and the wardrobe.* Normally only about half of their members and a few of the parents were expected for the break-up which was held on a Sunday. As a result of enthusiastic promotion of the puppet play, most of their regular children attended with many more of their parents than usual. This is a good indication of the drawing power of a puppet performance. Puppetry is unquestionably the most popular of all our methods of presentation from the children's point of view.

There is a wide variety of styles in puppet presentation and it is helpful to be aware of them. The first can be described as 'song and dance' and it's purpose is to entertain. The Muppet Show is the best example of this.

A second type is a form of slapstick where two character puppets hold a conversation to score points off each other. Bert and Ernie of 'Sesame Street' fame are a good example. While the apparent purpose of these puppets is to entertain, the underlying purpose is to impart knowledge. In the case of 'Sesame Street' the intention was to teach the alphabet and basic numbers.

Melodrama is a third form. A typical scenario might have a puppet popping up on stage and announcing to the audience that he is in a haunted house. He asks the group to call out and tell him if they happen to see a ghost. The character then turns to the side and a ghost puppet appears behind him. As requested the audience shriek out their warning but as the puppet turns back the ghost disappears and so on.

Drama is another method. In this the puppets act the part of characters in a story. Drama is entertainment, but it can also have a teaching purpose. Children who watch a dramatised Bible story, for example, remember it in minute detail as a result. One woman who purchased a script on the life of Gideon reported, 'We used your play on Gideon at our holiday club and I think it would be true to say that the children remember every detail of the events of Gideon's life.'

Rather than using a puppet to preach or to point out the moral in a story, I prefer to perform the story and then apply the message later. As well as differing types of puppetry there are different types of puppets, e.g. finger puppets, rod puppets, glove puppets, shadow puppets, muppets (i.e. mouth puppets) marionettes, ventriloquy dolls, etc. Each of these types are suited to different situations.

If you wish to attract a crowd in a shopping centre or similar venue then muppets are best, as you use them to react with the crowd and you can more easily adapt them to the situation than the puppets in a more structured presentation.

For a more settled situation glove puppets are best, especially for performing a play, as each puppeteer can use two puppets at a time and can change to other characters with comparative ease. In addition these puppets can be used by people who have never worked puppets before, especially if accompanied by a pre-recorded script.

A 'personality' puppet such as a ventriloquial doll can help in making announcements, leading choruses, discussing teaching, etc. In using a puppet in this way it is wise to maintain that the puppet is always a puppet. Avoid putting into the puppet's mouth claims such as 'God answers my prayers' or 'I asked the Lord Jesus to come into my heart', and so on as these are things that a puppet cannot do.

In after school mission or holiday club program puppet productions based on *The pilgrim's progress*, the C.S. Lewis Narnia stories, Patricia St. John's *Treasures of the snow*, etc, can be used in a serialised form. These have great appeal to children.

Some of the more complicated types of puppets such as rod puppets and marionettes require considerable practice to master the skill required to manipulate them.

True puppetry is theatre in miniature requiring similar skills in production, e.g. costumes, scenery, properties, sound and lighting. I recommend *Puppet drama: a complete illustrated guide* by Robert and Jill French, a recent book from Scripture Union. It contains detailed step-by-step instructions for making a simple hand puppet and a stage; advice on scriptwriting, performance and the above-mentioned aspects of production; and five complete play scripts accompanied by music, director's notes and suggestions for costumes, scenery and properties.

QUICK SKETCHING

I am not an artist, nor do I have any latent artistic talent, yet quick sketching is the aid I use more than any other. Sketching, I believe, has the edge on other visuals because the developing picture intrigues the audience. A sketched talk has more life than one based on flan-o-graph or flash cards.

Children frequently say to me, 'You can draw good!' I usually mutter something about not looking too closely at the pictures, knowing that my material cannot sustain close scrutiny, while recognising on the other hand that I can draw better than most ten year olds.

In the quick sketch the picture hints at the presence of objects rather than attempting to depict them. Some helpful hints follow.

Three Tricks

1. Draw it 'out of sight'

This skill was perfected by Norman Blake. Below is one of his sketches hinting at a lion behind a rock.

2. Draw it 'off the edge of the page'

A teacher of my acquaintance who had one of my children in her class asked me to show her how to draw horses. When I asked her the reason behind her request, she explained that my daughter had said to her, 'You can't draw horses like my daddy can!' I drew the following picture showing Phillip catching up with the Ethiopian's chariot.

I explained that the horse had just gone 'off the edge of the page'. 'But that's nonsense!' blurted my friend. 'Not really', I replied, 'my daughter wasn't being untruthful. She imagined the horse that isn't there'.

3. Draw it 'so far in the distance you can't tell what it is'

Elsewhere I have mentioned the story of Abraham's servant seeking a wife for Isaac, which involves a camel train. There is no way that I could ever draw a camel except as a distant dot on the far horizon, as shown in the sketch below. There are ten camels in the train. (Number ten is behind a dune.)

I wouldn't dare attempt to draw Zacchaeus up in the branches of a tree—I would be bound to make a mess of it. I can however draw two dots and say 'There's Zacchaeus peering through the branches'.

Sketching scenery

Items of scenery are comparatively easy to draw if you practise some standard pieces. You can build up your background picture from there. For example, hills are easy to draw. (See the sketches on the next page.) For your first 500 sets do not attempt to draw more than three hills. You will soon become proficient at ranges of hills in a variety of shapes. The line at the base of the hills divides background from foreground.

You can pop in some trees to make the scene interesting. Study these progressive steps in sketching a palm tree.

Most other items of outdoor scenery can be formed from a wiggly line as follows.

The wiggly line should not be too pointed or too rounded; it is free-flowing. Practise until you get it right.

Below are some features of the landscape which use this wiggly line as a basis.

The illustration below shows my standard city. The name may change but the city doesn't; it has been Jerusalem, Bethlehem, Jericho, Samaria, depending upon the incident being described.

Sketching people

Many of us hesitate to try sketching because we are afraid of drawing people. This fear can be easily overcome. The starting point is to draw match-men. As the name suggests, all you need to do is draw a match and add a shadow and a blob for the nose. The nose suggests which way the match-man is looking.

Stick men (or little Jetts) are simply match men with limbs.

Practise them in a variety of positions—they depend upon body movement for their life. As you grow more confident you can draw them without defining knees and elbows.

A further step in learning to sketch is to try your hand at Keith Thompson's cartoon characters. These depend upon the emotion depicted on their faces for their effect. Keith's book, *Sketch and tell*, published by Scripture Union, will help you get started. Keith has drawn the illustrations for some of the talk outlines in this book and he has the following advice to give.

'To draw a Bible cartoon character I simply draw a round shape and fill in a few lines to give the mood or character of the person I am talking about.
We are not trying to be artists—just to communicate an idea quickly through sketching and immediately go on with the story or Christian principle we are teaching. The sketch allows for a change of pace and is a visual on which to hang our message. A Chinese proverb says 'What you hear you may forget . what you see you will remember!' With a quick sketch, people will see and remember.
Everyone can draw a circle or blob (don't worry about the

shape of it too much, after all, we're all a little different!).

If you are using coloured chalk, pastel or felt pen then fill it in solid—it helps people to see your shape and looks more interesting. Use a light orange shade or fawn which has universal acceptance. Then add the simple lines.

Ears and hair. . .   or Jewish hat

Perhaps a beard.   Happy eyes

Sad eyes   a nose

Happy smile   normal   unhappy   crying

Angry   surprised   frightened   worried

Soldiers   Pharisee

The faces are the same for men and women, boys and girls—it is generally just the hair that changes, or facial hair. Good sketching!

QUIZ GAMES ON OHP

Before I owned an OHP I drew patterns such as snakes and ladders, or noughts and crosses on my drawing board to use as the basis for quizzes. I have now adapted these to the overhead projector. (See my book *Quiz games for the overhead projector* at your bookshop.)

Game plans of this type are fairly easy to invent and easy to prepare for OHP use. Here's one of mine which I have used constantly with considerable success.

Risk-all

Q5				Q1	Home	Q1
WOW		Q6				Q5
	Risk all				Risk all	
		Q3		Q6	WOW	
	Q5			Q3		
			Q5			
	OOPS		Q4		OOPS	Q4
S		Q3		Q3		S

To conduct a Risk-all quiz divide your group into two teams and choose a captain from each group. The captain's task is to move a marker for the team on the OHP. One of your helpers moves from team to team with a box containing numbered ping pong balls. As a child selects a number from the box, the captain moves the marker the appropriate number of places. If it stops on a Q square, the leader asks the team a quiz question. If a correct answer is given the marker is moved on the number of places indicated, e.g. Q5.

You will notice that even though the tracks that the markers follow are separate they each have similar traps. If a marker lands on 'Oops' then it drops down to the square below and takes the next move from there. If it lands on 'Wow!' it moves up to the row above.

Should the marker land on 'Risk-all', the captain must choose whether to 'risk all' on another question. If the risk-all option is chosen then for a successful answer the marker moves to 'Home' and the game is won. If a wrong answer is given then the marker moves back to the start and that team begins all over again.

REDEEMER

In its biblical sense redemption includes the concept of buying back out of slavery. Today, we are confronted constantly with stories of kidnapping and hijacking, where a ransom is demanded. You can use such incidents to explain to children the concept of redeeming through the payment of a ransom. Alternatively you can use the idea set out in the following talk outline.

Talk outline

If you haven't any money I can tell you where you can get some [Draw a band of yellow on your board and frame it with black. Write on it Money Lent.]

Some shops have 'Money Lent' painted on their awnings.

Usually the window is protected by a wire grille and there are all kinds of items on display: cameras, watches, jewellery, sports goods, cassette players, and so on. To borrow money you must leave some item of value as a guarantee that you will bring the money back [I usually use my watch to demonstrate].

Some months later you return to 'redeem', that is, 'buy back' the item you left there. After paying back the money you borrowed plus some interest which the money lender charges, you walk out of the shop with your watch or camera or whatever it was you left there. If you don't go back to redeem your valuable item, it then can be sold to someone else after the time limit has expired. [Write 'redeem' and 'buy back' on your board. The purpose of explaining this procedure is to give children an understanding of the word 'redeem'. I find they are intrigued by this information. It is unlikely that they will grasp the biblical concept of redemption unless they understand the term in its simplest sense first. Having done so, switch to an explanation of redemption as demonstrated in Leviticus 25. Sketch two people as you speak].

Back in the days when the very early parts of the Bible were written many people had slaves who did all their work for them. There were different ways that you could become a slave. Perhaps you were captured during a war and the conquerors would take you back to their own country and make you their slave.

Or if a man borrowed money from someone and was unable to pay the money back, his creditor could take him as payment and make him his slave. He would put an iron collar around his neck [sketch it in], clip on a long chain [sketch it], and march him away as a slave [write 'slave' above him]. The slave wasn't happy [draw sad features on his face], but there was nothing he could do as that was what the law allowed. The other man of course was very pleased [draw smile on his face], as he was now the owner or Master of the other man [write 'master' above him].

SLAVE   MASTER
me   sin

Before I tell you how this man could get out of this fix, let me bring all of you into my story. This man with the chain around his neck is a picture of me and a picture of you. [Write 'me' above him.]

We haven't any chains around our necks but we are still slaves. You might not agree with that. You might want to argue that you aren't a slave to anybody. Listen to what the Bible says about slavery. 'Everyone who sins is a slave of sin' (John 8:34). [Write 'sin' beside 'master'.]

Let me show you how sin is our master. The teacher is busy working at her desk and you whisper something to your friend.

'Were you talking?' asks the teacher.

'No miss!' you reply.

Because she isn't sure whether you talked or not she has to let you off. Telling lies can get us out of trouble. When New Years' Day comes around you say to yourself, 'I don't like being a liar, I'll make a New Year Resolution never to tell lies again.' How long is that likely to last? A day! Five minutes! Two seconds! [The children will give you a variety of answers.] Telling lies has become a habit that is too hard to break. Sin has become our master.

In Bible times a man who had become a slave due to debt could be redeemed if someone paid a sum of money. [As you speak sketch a third figure holding a money bag.] In fact only relatives had the right to do this—a right given by the Law (Leviticus 25:49). [Write 'Relative' above the figure.] A friend's offer to pay could be refused.

RELATIVE

Do you know why Jesus became a human? When he became one of us, our relative, it gave him the right to redeem us out of slavery to sin.

Of course money couldn't pay for our redemption. If we lumped together all the money in the world it would not be enough. Jesus gave something much more valuable than that. Let me give you a clue. [Sketch a cross.] Who can tell me what was the price he paid? [If the children say 'his death' explain that when he died, there was something he gave up. Write up 'His Life'.]

Why did Jesus give his life for us? [Answer—to redeem us from slavery to sin.]

Why did Jesus need to give his life for us? [Answer— Because all of us had sinned.]

What Jesus wants us to do is to put our trust in what he has done for us. When we do so, he can set us free from sin's control so that we are able to live for him.

(See *What happens if a Christian sins*)

RESEARCHING BIBLE STORIES

What makes a Bible talk work? What is it that captures the audience? Enthusiasm, participation, relevance, visuals? All of these deserve a place on a list of ten; however, I would put 'content' on the top of the list. People of all ages need to discover from you something that is important, exciting, illuminating—something they can chew over.

On some occasions I have visited schools expecting to speak for thirty minutes to discover that the period lasts for forty minutes. At other times I have been allocated twenty five minutes and I have completed all that I intended to say in fifteen! It can be fatal trying to bluff the class into continuing to be interested for an extended time when you have *nothing to say of any consequence.*

Thus it is particularly important when preparing a Bible story to be accurate and thorough. Failure to do this can be disastrous.

One of my beach mission team members was given the task of speaking on the story of Absalom's rebellion. When he began to speak it soon became obvious that he had not checked the story but was relying on his memory. He became hopelessly muddled. The error he made was to put Joab, who was the general in charge of David's forces, on the wrong side. If you are familiar with this incident you will appreciate something of the confusion that this created. To make matters worse, he didn't know where he had gone wrong and he floundered on, recounting a story that became more fictitious with every sentence.

What do we do when people are already very familiar with the story? Children often complain that the teaching at Sunday school is the 'same old thing'. 'We've heard this one before!' is the chorus. This is especially so at Easter or Christmas. The great truths of the gospel story seem to lose their power because children can become bored through familiarity. Sunday school teachers, for their part, have often told me that they have considerable difficulty teaching their group because they 'already know it all'. My reply is, 'No, they don't! It's just that you must dig more deeply into the Bible story to come up with information that is unfamiliar to them.' The following guidelines will help you dig.

1. Take careful note of all of the details

Many of us skim across the surface of Bible stories and ignore much of the finer detail. Take for example the incident of the Lord Jesus calming the storm. How much detail can you remember? At a meeting of the leaders of your children's club, split up into two groups. Ask group A to record as much of the story as they can from memory and ask Group B to make a list using their Bibles. Generally the list that Group B compiles is fuller and more accurate than that compiled by those who are relying on their memories. Yet, I have been intrigued to note that frequently this group overlook some of the details in front of them.

Mark's account of this incident is the fullest (Mark 4:35–41). Let's see how much detail there is for us to exploit in this incident.

- The journey began in the evening, v.35.
- The Lord had been using the boat to preach from and was already in it, v.36.
- A number of other boats accompanied them, v.36.
- Jesus fell asleep in the stern of the boat lying on a cushion, v.38.
- A furious storm arose, v.37.
- The waves broke over the boat, v.37.
- They were in danger of being swamped, v.37.
- The disciples woke Jesus up roughly, v.38.
- 'Don't you care if we drown?' they said, v.38.
- Jesus stood up, v.39.
- He rebuked the storm with the words, 'Quiet, be still', v.39.
- The wind died away and everything became completely calm, v.39.
- Jesus rebuked the disciples for their lack of faith, v.40.
- The disciples were terrified by this display of supernatural power, v.41.
- They asked each other, 'Who is this?' Even the wind and the waves obey him!' v.41.

It all seems fairly familiar, doesn't it? What facts from this summary had you previously overlooked? The time of the day the journey began? The presence of other boats? The cushion? The disciples' terror at the display of Jesus' power?

2. Take note of the context in which the story is reported

What did the Lord teach from the incident involving the crowd of more than five thousand people? This question can only be answered by studying the latter section of John's account (John 6). He reports that Jesus rebuked the crowd for following 'not because you saw miraculous signs but because you ate the loaves and had your fill.' He warns them of the futility of spending their energies for things that don't last and makes sure they know that he himself is 'the bread of life' that satisfies their needs.

I'm sure you will agree that John's version adds significantly to our understanding of the incident.

3. Trace subsequent references to the story

For new light on Old Testament storie seek out New Testament references to them.

When some boys from a Crusader group invited me to speak at their meeting the school chaplain rang me, explained that they were currently following a series on the life of Moses and asked me to base my address on the next section. I agreed to do so and asked which passage it was. He explained that it was the section relating to Moses killing the Egyptian slave driver and fleeing from Egypt.

'You know what you can tell them,' he said, 'Moses was impetuous and acted on his own volition instead of waiting for God's leading. As a result he had to be disciplined by spending forty years in the desert where God moulded his character and turned him into leadership material.'

Much of what the chaplain said was familiar as I had found a similar emphasis in Sunday School lesson books. Yet to my surprise I discovered not even a hint of this when I examined the text. Moses may have been a better leader as a result of his desert experience but the reason for the additional forty years of slavery that the Israelites endured was their rejection of his leadership. While this is not obvious if we read Exodus chapter two in isolation, it leaps at us from the page when we turn to Stephen's speech in Acts chapter seven. My address to the boys at that Crusader group had an entirely different emphasis from that which the chaplain had suggested.

Further light may be thrown on some incidents, particularly Old Testament stories, if you seek out reference to them in later chapters or books. For example, in Genesis 37 we read of Joseph's brothers attacking him, stripping him of his robe and throwing him into a pit. There is no indication of Joseph's reaction to this treatment. Did he protest? Did he fight? Did he plead with them? Yes he did, but we must turn to chapter 42 verse 21 to discover this fact. There the brothers say to one another: 'Surely we are being punished because of our brother. We saw how distressed he was when he pleaded with us for his life, but we would not listen.'

When we come to the Gospels, the raising of Lazarus (John 11:1-44) is related at length but it is important to notice that the story doesn't stop there. In the next chapter it is recorded that the Lord paid another visit to his friends in Bethany, and that Lazarus was one of those who shared the meal with him. Isn't it ironic that the chief priests were plotting the death of Lazarus? He was an annoyance to them, walking proof of the power of Jesus. We're not finished with the Lazarus incident even then, as a further reference to it is made in the account of the triumphal entry (12:17). The raising of Lazarus had a profound effect on the people who witnessed it. They were able to answer those who were puzzled by the Lord's arrival (Matthew 21:10). In fact it was their report that had brought many of the people onto the streets to join the jubilant welcome in the first place (John 12:18).

SIN

Sin is an important biblical theme. It's the Bible's label for the picture we see everywhere around us. It's the big picture we see in every daily newspaper and it's also the small picture we see when we look at ourselves honestly. But without this bad news, the Bible's good news would have no meaning. Our teaching must therefore include an explanation of sin. How do we go about explaining this theological concept to children?

Children are usually realistic about the wrong they see and do. Little children will not understand 'sin' in the full biblical sense—but they will readily understand that they are sometimes good and sometimes naughty. As they grow older, so also their understanding of life, the world and the reality of sin and evil should become more mature.

We need not dwell on the subject of sin every time we meet with children, but we do need to be realistic and serious about the effect of sin in our lives and God's commitment to forgiving us and freeing us from its power. At heart, sin is rebellion. It is refusal to accept God's right to rule our lives and a desire to go our own way instead. Sin is not only 'doing wrong' but also 'not doing right'. When we teach children that sin is 'doing wrong' they are very often unperturbed—after all 'everyone does it'. Our teaching must therefore include an explanation of sin. It is significant that our Lord places stress upon the sins of omission. Consider for example the parable of the Ten Bridesmaids and the parable of the talents in Matthew 25 where the principal characters failed.

Ask children which sin they consider to be the very worst and nine times out of ten they will say murder. It is fairly safe to assume that none of them have committed murder and that they are unlikely to do so. Yet, they may all be guilty of hatred, springing from jealousy and leading them to be spiteful. Take notice of the way children behave towards each other and you will soon find practical examples with which to illustrate your talk.

The fact of sin on its own, however, isn't good news but very bad news. At Scripture Union's stand at the Royal Easter Show we performed a puppet play based on the Jungle Doctor parable of the snake that stole the eggs. We were thrilled to see a crowd collect each time it was performed. Yet in a discussion after the show, those of us who were involved in its preparation agreed that we had failed to present the gospel. The message of the story, which I'm sure Dr. Paul White never intended to be used in isolation as we had done, was 'You can't sin and get away with it'. There's no good news in that! The following year we performed a biblical play called *Jesus is alive*. The message of the play's title came through very clearly in the text and all agreed that the gospel had been faithfully presented.

Whenever we talk about sin and show the way it spoils our lives, we must make sure we also comprehensively cover the other grand themes of the Bible: God's grace, the way God forgives and rescues people and how we can be reconciled to God.

SINGING

'Isn't he great?' said the Sunday School superintendent. 'The children love his music! Since he joined us we don't do anything else in our opening session. We sing, have an opening prayer, take up the offertory and then break for classes'. While I had to agree that the guitarist was one of the best I had heard and the singing was really rocking along, I had my doubts about the wisdom of the way they had structured their program. The following day my doubts were confirmed. Children were straggling past the hall on their way home from school.

'Are you coming to the meeting this afternoon?' I asked some boys.

The boys stopped.

'What's on?' one of them asked.

'We've got some special meetings for boys and girls every day this week', I replied. 'I think you would enjoy them if your mother would let you come.'

'D'ya 'ave a lotta that singin' there?' asked the boy.

My mind whirled like a top—something about the tone of his voice alerted me. 'Singing, well a bit, but not much! We have puzzles and puppets and stories and prizes and games, and. . .'

By the time I had completed the list the boys were showing much more interest. They hurried away to get permission to attend. Bright singing can be an attractive feature of the program but too much of it becomes tedious.Here are some guidelines for selecting songs.

(a) Select most of the songs you intend to use beforehand rather than leaving it to the 'Who's got a favourite chorus' approach.

(b) Remember 'familiarity breeds contempt'. In a holiday club, my intention is to teach a new song every day rather than singing those songs with which the children are familiar. In a more regular activity such as an after school club I suggest you set the target of learning a new song once a month.

(c) Avoid duplication. By this I mean that you should have music that is the hallmark of your club rather than using the same songs the children sing in Sunday School.

(d) Vary the style of song. Rather than allowing the singing to be dominated by the more rollicking type of song, include some with a more lilting refrain especially just before the children's talk.

STOPPING WHEN YOU FINISH!

In my childhood we sang a little ditty:

Oh Jemima, look at your Uncle Clive,
He's in the garage learning how to drive.
First he is in low gear, then he is in top
Now he's racing down the street
Wondering how to stop.

How many times have you heard a speaker who seemed to be having a similar problem?

Everyone knows that children have short attention spans. The younger the child the shorter the time you can expect them to concentrate. Despite our awareness of this, many of us drag on ad infinitum, not knowing when to leave off. Yet to launch into a lengthy explanation or interpretation is a sure way to kill their interest. Rather than tacking on an application at the end of a talk or Bible story, we need to weave it into the structure of the story itself. A pill is easier to swallow if it is mashed up and mixed with honey.

In my book *Visualised Bible stories for the overhead projector*, the story of the healing of Blind Bartimaeus employs this principle. To begin, a picture of an old coat lying in a city gateway is projected onto the OHP screen. The story opens by mentioning the litter in our streets e.g. old car bodies down the back lanes, and scattered pieces of tyres by the roadsides. The speaker then draws attention to the picture of the coat and explains that it used to belong to a blind beggar called Bartimaeus. As the figure representing Bartimaeus is moved into the scene, it blocks out the picture of the coat.

The story is related up to the point where Bartimaeus is helped to his feet to meet Jesus. As the seated figure of Bartimaeus is moved, the picture of the old coat is revealed.

'The Bible tells us that when Bartimaeus went to meet Jesus he left his coat behind. He must have had really strong faith. A blind man can't leave his coat behind and find it again unless he is able to see again.'

At this point the speaker brings in the application, pointing out that Bartimaeus had sufficient knowledge of who Jesus was to believe that he could do the impossible and restore his eyesight. Notice that in this way the story is interrupted at one of its peaks, not in a lull.

After this interruption the speaker picks up the flow of the story again, reporting the conversation between Bartimaeus and the Lord Jesus followed by the climactic moment when the blind man's sight is restored. The conclusion then picks up again on the coat.

'I wonder whether Bartimaeus went back to pick up his coat. Maybe he was so eager to follow Jesus that he forgot about it'. Maybe passers-by saw the coat lying there and said, "Say, isn't that Bartimaeus's old coat? He must have forgotten it. Wasn't it amazing that Jesus was able to heal him. Jesus really must be the Son of God." '

Notice the flow of this outline: it focuses on an obscure detail, the coat, and uses it to link the introduction, the application and the conclusion. Plan your conclusion. Know what your final words are going to be, say them, then stop. A good conclusion satisfies the expectations aroused at the beginning.

TEMPO OF CHILDREN'S MEETINGS

Children thrive on variety, so pack into your program as many different features as possible. The tempo of a good children's meeting can be described as 'unhurried haste'. Move briskly from one item to another, avoiding anything that drags. As a rough guide, each section of the overall program should be limited to approximately ten minutes; the exception may be the talk that you can give which could stretch to a quarter of an hour.

If you have a team of helpers, each participant should know

when to come on and how long their segment is to take so that the whole meeting flows smoothly. When a number of people are participating the golden rule is never leave the platform empty. As one person leaves, another must be ready to take over. Your role as leader is to keep everything flowing smoothly.

Train your team not to dither. Each person should start straight in on the segment of the program that has been allocated to them and not hark back to something that has previously happened.

If you have a visitor to introduce, don't gush! As one who has spent years as a visiting speaker at a variety of children's functions I assure you that nothing is more likely to make my task of getting the attention of the children difficult than the leader who takes five minutes to tell the children what a wonderful speaker I am and how privileged they are having me come to visit them.

Another very off-putting introduction is when the leader warns the children to be on their best behaviour, or else. This is mainly a failure of headmasters and other school staff members and is an unconscious vote of no-confidence in the visitor's ability to interest the children.

UNDERSTANDING CHILDREN

Jesus called a little child and had him stand among them. And he said, 'I tell you the truth, unless you change and become like little children you will never enter the kingdom of heaven.' At face value that is a very simple statement, yet it has been the subject of thousands of sermons and many hours of intense discussion. What does it mean to be 'like little children?'

What are little children like? While you don't need a degree in child psychology to take on the responsibility of teaching children, you do need some basic insights into what they are like if you wish to communicate with them successfully.

Eavesdropping

Watching children and listening to them is the best way to find out what makes them tick.

One of the founders of Scripture Union, Tom Bishop, always made a point of 'eavesdropping' on groups of children. He was an alert observer. This enabled him to know what activities were of interest to children, so that he could design magazines to suit their needs. He was obviously on the children's wavelength, because those early Scripture Union magazines had a huge circulation.

As well as observing children, watch those workers who appear to be successful in capturing and maintaining the interest of children. Do not assume that they are more gifted than you are. While this may be true to some extent, their secret is that they have developed skills that you can learn. Try to analyse what they do and why—it may help you to become more competent in your communication with children.

Watch children's television, in particular those programs which children talk about. This enables you to join in their conversation. Without being judgmental about what they watch, you can sometimes ask children 'Do you think that was right?' This can help them think about some of the moral standards that underlie what they see on the screen.

Friendship

Most adults ignore the presence of children. Those with children of their own may not necessarily be interested in other children. Even in children's activities such as camps and after-school clubs it is possible for adult workers to associate more with the other team members than with the children themselves. The best children's workers, however, are those who are prepared to spend the maximum amount of time with the children. Mixing with children is the quickest way to learn about them.

The first step is to be able to converse with children. Unless you feel comfortable doing this, you will find it difficult to relax and be informal when helping them discover how to trust and follow Jesus.

Plan extra activities for your class or group such as a trip to a zoo, museum or other place of interest to gain further insights into what makes them tick. Friends of mine borrowed some of my camping gear and took the boys from their Sunday school classes for a week-end bushwalk.

'It was terrific!' they told me. 'We seem to have got to know the boys so much better as a result.'

One young Sunday school teacher at a training conference described the predicament he found himself in. He had been allocated a mixed class of fourteen year olds who informed him in their first lesson that they only attended Sunday school because of pressure from their parents. They went on to state quite bluntly that they didn't want to learn what he wanted to teach them and that he was wasting his time trying.

What advice would you give to someone in that predicament? All I could suggest was that he do his utmost to establish a friendship with each individual child. He could find out if any were involved in sporting teams and make time to watch them play and cheer them on. He could question them about their hobbies and other interests to find some common links. Showing that he was interested in them as individuals might help to break down their antagonism.

Children and young people respond positively to warmth and friendship. One of the reasons given by children who drop out of Sunday school is that they 'didn't like the teacher'. Perhaps the teacher was unwilling to give them the acceptance and friendship they desired. Befriending children does not come naturally to many of us and we must make a conscious effort to make ourselves available to them.

The following incident brought this home to me. My phone

rang and the caller explained that as a child he was orphaned and spent nine years in the Burnside Homes. During that time Scripture Union teams visited the homes every week to conduct Sunday school.

'One of the teachers was a man named Henderson, he was kind to me. I would like to know how to contact him.' I was able to put them in touch with each other.

Remember your own childhood

Did you like pumpkin when you were a child? I certainly didn't. If you are planning the menu for a children's camp, keep in mind the things you disliked as a child. You can be fairly confident that many of the children will have similar likes and dislikes today. The same goes for any of your work with children: put yourself in the children's shoes. To be able to recall the feelings you had as a child will be a real asset in your ministry. One area where adults often show a lack of sensitivity towards children is public prayer. I am puzzled by Christians who as children hated people praying long prayers, but now inflict on children the very same thing.

Amongst the children you are teaching there are probably some who are similar to what you were like when you were a child. One boy who was a regular at our camps was always up to mischief but I was consistently able to thwart his pranks. Finally, in exasperation, he said, 'How do you always know what we're going to do?'

'I have my ways,' I replied non-committally. After all, how could I have explained to him that he was the same type of boy I had been? I could think his thoughts before him!

(See *Breaking the ice; Curiosity*)

VENUE

In planning a children's rally or meeting, it is important to prepare the venue well. The wise children's worker will arrive early and check all aspects. Six things come to mind immediately.

1. Tidiness

A critical stranger would be quick to point out the tattered out-of-date posters on the walls, the untidy heap of posters stacked behind the piano and the junk that litters the top of the cupboard. Such untidiness may go unnoticed by adults familiar with the surroundings, but children will find it dist-racting.

2. Ventilation

This contributes significantly to the comfort of your audience. A large group in a confined space can rapidly create a heaviness in the atmosphere unless there is adequate air-flow. Obviously in summer you will leave all the windows open but even in winter it is wise to leave some open.

3. Lighting

Avoid lights behind the speaker as they can have a hypnotic effect. Spotlights are also inadvisable as they make it difficult for the speaker to see the audience.

4. Amplification

Many halls are wired for sound but never assume that everything is in working order; check it beforehand. If you are using your own amplification equipment remember to locate the speakers as high as possible so that the sound travels across your group.

Additional speakers are essential with large groups. Cassette players which appear to punch out ample volume when the hall is empty turn out to be inadequate when the hall is full of sound absorbing bodies.

5. Layout

We are all familiar with the order given by many a captain: 'Don't shoot till you can see the whites of their eyes'. Closeness to your audience is important in children's work; it is unwise to speak from a high pulpit or platform. It may even be necessary to construct a temporary platform at a lower level to enable you to move closer to your group.

If the meeting is held out of doors in a park or on the beach, plan the positioning of the group with care. Avoid seating the children so that they are looking into the sun as this will make it difficult for them to give you their attention. Check the direction of the prevailing wind and choose a site where the wind carries your voice across the crowd. Speaking into the wind places unnecessary strain both on the speaker's voice and the audiences' ears.

6. Seating

Only set out seating for the number you anticipate; it is easy for your helpers to move more in if your estimated number is exceeded. When arranging seating, make sure that all seats are positioned so that everyone in the audience can see clearly. In groups that cover a wide age range it is wise to bring the small children down to the front rows where they will be able to see more clearly. Bring the rows closer together than you would normally allow for adults—children do not need as much leg room. Avoid seating children side on to each other where they can see others in the group as this will be a source of distraction.

On some occasions it may be appropriate for children to sit on the floor; however, if this proves uncomfortable, they will become restless. Chairs are preferable if the meeting lasts an hour.

VISI-WHEEL STORY

Never seen a visi-wheel? It's simple really! It is designed to be used with an overhead projector. Below is an example of a visi-wheel story. It focuses on the emotions of the people who were present at the crucifixion of Jesus.

The visi-wheel is used with an OHP transparency made in the usual way (see *Overhead projectors*). First, enlarge the illustration on page 172 to fill an A4 sheet of paper. Then go through the following steps.

Making a visi-wheel

1. Mark out a circle on a piece of cardboard, and mark five segments as shown in the adjacent diagram. Draw dotted lines on each side of the lines which form the segments, at a distance of about 5 millimetres, from the centre of the circle to the edge. Cut out the segments along the dotted lines. The strips of cardboard betwen the segments will look like the spokes of a wheel and will provide stability. This is your base card.

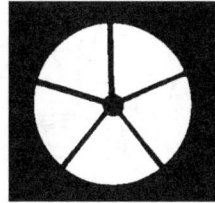

2. Cut out a second circle slightly larger than the first, and cut out just one segment from it.

3. Mount the transparency on the base card, with the spokes uppermost. Take care to line up the spokes of the visi-wheel with the gaps between the pictures, so that nothing is missing when the pictures appear on the screen. Secure with masking tape.

4. Place the second wheel on top. A winged paper clip through the axis of both cards will allow you to move the wheel over each of the pictures in turn.

Talk outline

[Begin by discussing emotion and the way we reveal what we feel by the look on our faces. Here's your opportunity to practise pulling funny faces.]

When we're happy, we look like this [Smile]

When we're angry, we look like this [Scowl]

When we're bored. . .etc.

When Jesus was crucified a large crowd of people gathered on the hill outside the city to watch him die (Luke 23:27). Why were they there?

Many of them were like this man. [Switch on first face.]

They went to jeer. [Describe the crowd and graphically re-enact the scene by repeating their ridicule. See Luke 23:35, Mark 15:29-32, Matthew 27:39-43. Discuss with your class why it was that these people were so antagonistic towards Jesus. John 19:7, Matthew 27:18.]

There are people like them today.

Some were there because it was their job. [Show the second picture and describe the soldiers who divided up his clothes and gambled for his undergarments. John 19:23-24.] These men just couldn't care less. From their point of view the crucifixion of Jesus was nothing to do with them. They were only interested in what they could get out of it. The one who won the toss and went home with Jesus' coat must have been very pleased. I wonder how long it lasted before it wore out.

A few of the people who were there at the cross were very distressed. [Show the picture of Mary and recount the incident described in John 19:25-27, see also Mark 15:40.]

As Mary stood there she may have remembered the warning given to her by the prophet Simeon, at the time of Jesus' birth, Luke 2:35.

There were some who didn't want to be there at all. The two thieves who were crucified at the same time would rather have been anywhere else but there. [Show the fourth picture. Des-cribe the conversation reported in Luke 23:39-43. Point out that to begin with both men sneered at Jesus, Matthew 27:44. At this point you can explain the purpose of Jesus' death pointing out that the repentant thief was forgiven and given the promise that he would be 'with' Jesus.]

We too can experience forgiveness if we are willing to put our trust in him. There was at least one person at the crucifixion who came to realise who Jesus is: The centurion who was in charge of the squad of soldiers. [Show the final picture. Describe a centurion's responsibilities.]

'When the centurion who stood there in front of Jesus, heard his cry and saw how he died he said, "Surely this man was the Son of God" ', Mark 15:39. [Compare Matthew 27:50-54; Luke 23:44-47.]

Although you live many centuries after the event took place, what are your feelings as you are reminded of what the Lord Jesus has done for you?

[Try to encourage a mood that will help the children to think about this story. Encourage them to be quiet with their eyes closed (not for prayer but for imagining) while you quietly talk about the characters in your story, and their response to Jesus. Ask the children to think about whether there is one character who is most like them, but don't ask for a public response. Encourage the children to silently talk to God about how they feel about the death of the Lord Jesus.]

VISUAL AIDS

Wander around a foodhall in any large shopping centre and you will be amazed at the range of food on offer: Indian and Thai curry, Chinese chop suey, Japanese sushi, Indonesian nasi goreng, English roast beef, French pastries, Lebanese homous and tabouleh, hamburgers. Cooks know the truth of the saying, 'Variety is the spice of life'.

Variety in presenting the gospel message, especially to children, is vitally important too. The children who have dropped out of Sunday School, children's clubs and so on, say that they did so because it was boring. Boredom can be prevented if you imaginatively utilise the many aids that are available. There are a number of reasons for including visuals in your presentation.

1. Visuals attract attention

If you stand on a street corner and stare up at a high rise building, passers-by will inevitably stop and glance up to see what it is you are staring at. Erect a puppet theatre in a shopping centre and a crowd will gather even before you begin your performance. People are basically curious and if we can arouse their curiosity we will be able to communicate with them more effectively.

2. Visuals awaken interest

You must, in the first instance, have something interesting to say, but you must also present this information in an interesting way. A visual presentation not only awakens interest but also helps maintain it throughout.

A Scripture teacher built a portable shadow puppet screen and used it to give the lesson to her class, who gave her their rapt attention. At the conclusion of the period one of the boys said to her, 'It's much better when you've got something to show us. Much better than when you just stand up there and talk.'

3. Visuals assist understanding

The biblical era seems light years away from our time. If the children we teach have never seen a sheep, then lessons about lost sheep may be confusing to them. Imagine trying to describe a banana to people who had never seen one. ' Well—er—it's a fruit. It's yellow with a black tip at each end. It's shaped like a half-moon or um-ah-a sort of a hook.' After hear-ing this your audience will still be in the dark. On the other hand if you pass around some bananas so that your class can see them, touch them, smell them and taste them, they will soon know as much as you do about bananas.

Long descriptions of life in Bible times are terribly boring. An object, a model or a picture can quickly solve the problem for you.

4. Visuals aid the memory

'We used a puppet play on Gideon at our holiday club and the children remember the story down to the finest detail.' If you want your class to retain the lesson use a visual presentation. 'The eye remembers long after the ear has forgotten.'

Guidelines for producing visual aids

'Can you all see that?' asked the youth worker, as he projected up the words of a Christmas carol. 'No', chorused those who were at the back of the congregation. 'Oh-er-well, you'll probably know it. If you don't, do your best to follow the rest of us!' was his embarrassed reply. This type of poor presentation is far too common. It can be improved if the following simple principles are followed.

1. Visuals must be clear

(a) Size
   If your visual isn't large enough to be seen by those in the back row in your class, it ought not to be used at all. Nothing frustrates your audience more than a visual that is too small. This is particularly true when using an overhead projector. The minimum size for lettering should be 36 point (a printing measurement which is the equivalent of 12.5mm).

(b) Colour
   'Whenever someone projects up printing done with green ink I have to put my glasses on!' Generally, black letter-

ing is best, though strong colours such as royal blue or crimson may be satisfactory. Colour is appealing, but be careful—its incorrect use can detract from, rather than enhance, the clarity of your material.

(c) *Printing*

Probably due to filling out government forms, adults have a habit of printing in capitals. This is not what children are taught at school. Discipline yourself to print in lower case.

(d) *Neatness*

Simple things such as cutting the paper you use to the size of your board will enhance your presentation. Never be content with a slip-shod, half-hearted effort. Look critically at what you do and if you think you can do better, start again. Remember Colossians 3:24, 'It is the Lord Christ you are serving.'

2. Visuals must be simple

(a) *Wording*

I recall seeing a beach missioner give a talk based on an acrostic on the word 'Christmas'. Each letter was printed on a card which one of the children held up. I cannot recall any of the points he made. A nine point sermon was too wordy to retain.

(b) *Structure*

Many of us know the embarrassment of having too many cards or pieces of equipment that somehow get muddled up as the talk progresses. We can prevent this happening if we follow the 'kiss' principle (Keep It Simple Stupid). If a visual draws attention to itself it can detract from the impact of the message. A friend with quick sketching skills began using luminous chalk which shone like a neon sign when a 'black light' was switched on. So many people approached him to ask how he achieved this effect that he went back to using demonstration chalk. At the point where he wanted his audience to ponder the truth of his message, they were being distracted by the visual aid.

(c) Space

Be careful not to produce visuals that look cluttered. The pictures you draw do not need a lot of detail; 'simplicity assists clarity'.

3. Visuals must be suitable

(a) For the age group

What sense is there in holding up a printed chart if the children are too young to be able to read it? Even when they are old enough to read there may be words and concepts that are beyond them. On the other hand, visuals that are suitable for infants and primaries may be 'kids stuff' to teenagers. Keep alert and you will soon sense whether your visual is unsuitable.

(b) For the generation

Would you believe that less than fifty years ago slide pro- jectors used three inch square glass slides? The projectors were called 'magic lanterns'. Technologically, the world is changing at an alarming rate; what is commonplace today is obsolete tomorrow. The challenge to those of us who wish to communicate through visual presentation is— keep up!

4. Visuals can be original

(a) Imaginative

Those visuals that I have produced from my own imag- ination have given me the most satisfaction. One of the ᵇᵉnefits of the quick sketching technique is that you can ᵃam up your own pictures rather than only using pre- ᵈ ones.

(b) Home-made

One of the constant complaints of Scripture teachers is that they aren't made of money. Flan-o-graph, OHP stories, puppets, audio visuals, videos all involve expense, either to hire or purchase. Home-made materials can in fact be just as effective. Let's be honest—the reason why we prefer ready made material that is pre-drawn, pre-cut, etc, is that it saves us work. Why not use some of the skilled teenagers who attend your church to help you produce your own visuals?

5. Visuals should be varied

You can use visuals to:
- display the words of songs
- teach memory texts
- enhance quizzes
- illustrate talks

Utilise as many visual tools as you can: quick sketching, flash cards, pictures, flan-o-graph, objects, maps, diagrams, puppets, films, etc. You cannot overdo the use of visuals. They help to make your message memorable.

WHAT HAPPENS IF A CHRISTIAN SINS?

'I prayed that prayer you told me about but it didn't work!' said a ten year old at a GFS meeting.

'Oh! Why do you say that?' I asked.

'I got into trouble for talking in class today,' she replied.

When we are preaching enthusiastically about forgiveness and freedom from the power of sin, etc, it is possible for children to get the impression that once they put their trust in the Lord they will be sinless and perfect. We need to give them some guidance as to how to cope with failure. When we consciously lie or cheat, or are envious or proud, we lose our joy, our peace and our witness; but not our salvation.

ollowing conversation was reported to me by a Sunday eacher who was involved with following up a decision that one of her class had made. It took place about six months after the mission I conducted.

Girl: 'I'm not a Christian any more.'

Teacher: 'Oh! Why, what has happened?'

Girl: 'I did something very naughty.'

Teacher: 'I see. Er, where are you living now?'

Girl: 'At home!'

Teacher: 'Don't your parents know about the naughty thing you did?'

Girl: 'Yes, they know.'

Teacher: 'And didn't they tell you to leave home because of that?'

Girl: 'Of course not! I belong to their family!'

Teacher: 'If you belong to God's family do you think he would be any different?'

She went on to explain how we can ask the Lord for forgiveness and strength to resist temptation.

WORDS THAT CAPTIVATE

Words are the building blocks of storytelling and your choice of words is significant to your success in involving and delighting your hearers. When relating Bible stories, get into the habit of using colourful words. Vivid, evocative and unusual words help them to picture mentally the events described. For example, rather than 'said', any of the following words are more colourful: mumbled, muttered, stammered, stuttered, grumbled, grizzled, whinged, whispered, shouted, chattered. Again, how much more appealing are 'gobbled' and 'gulped' than 'ate'. Instead of merely 'walking', a character could stride, rush, amble, trudge, march, tiptoe, stagger or slink.

You can create an exciting effect by stringing together a set of descriptive adjectives. For example: King Nebuchadnezzar made a great big, enormous, tremendous, stupendous, fantastic, magnificent image! This type of effect can be heightened with the use of alliteration, for example: Down in the deepest, darkest, dingiest, dirtiest, dampest dungeon in Jerusalem was a man in chains. Practice rolling all those 'd' words off your tongue as though you were repeating a tongue twister and you'll see what I mean.

Become alert to the words used in good children's literature. Learn from expert writers, but be a critical observer and develop a personal style of your own that feels comfortable.

Suit your language to your audience, avoiding terms and phrases that are over the heads of children. It is especially important to use the colloquial language of everyday conversation. For example, these days Australians would never say, 'He scorned it' but rather 'He rubbished it'. The latter borders on slang, but more importantly, it is a phrase that children today would be familiar with. Most authors writing on public speaking, oppose the use of slang but I use a fair degree of it, and I think it can be helpful providing you use expressions common in everyday speech. Do not use slang, however, to impress your audience; children won't understand what you are trying to do, while teenagers will despise your efforts to ingratiate yourself to them. Words should not attract attention to themselves, but to the ideas that they express. Diction and pronunciation have an important part to play in verbal communication and I would encourage you to include in your personal library some books on public speaking and speech in ral.

e *Dialogue in storytelling*)

ZACCHAEUS

A look at the well known story of Zacchaeus (Luke 19) illustrates the need to work thoroughly through the biblical material and then to think carefully about the words we use with children.

The crowd who overheard the Lord say that he wished to have a meal with Zacchaeus criticised Jesus for going 'to be the guest of a sinner'. Instantly the question arises, what is a sinner? When Zacchaeus declared his intention to give half of his goods to the poor and pay back those he had cheated, Jesus declared 'Salvation has come to this man's house'. There's another of those difficult words cropping up. What is salvation?

We aren't finished yet. Jesus went on to say that Zacchaeus was 'a son of Abraham'. What is a 'son of Abraham'? I have heard many groups singing with great enthusiasm,

'Father Abraham had many sons,
Many sons had Father Abraham.
I am one of them and so are you,
So let's all praise the Lord'.

Without being unkindly critical let me say that most, if not all of the children, and many of the teachers had no idea what these lyrics mean. (To discover the answer, turn to Galatians 3:6-7.)

The title 'Son of Man' (verse 10) is one that the theologians have haggled over for years. Happily children will accept that this title was a way Jesus described himself and we can ignore any theological difficulties it presents. Finally in verse 10 we have 'to seek and to save what was lost'. Even the word 'lost' stands for an abstract idea. Zacchaeus wasn't lost in the sense of not knowing his way home; he was lost in the social sense that his self-centredness had caused a barrier between himself and the people who would not associate with him, and also in the spiritual sense that it had cut him off from God.

'Sinner', 'salvation', 'son of Abraham', 'son of Man' and 'lost' make quite a collection of difficult terms from a story as well known as that of Zacchaeus. To throw these terms at children indiscriminately is to erect unnecessary hurdles in the way of their understanding the point of the story. Introduce explanations of these concepts as you go along.

(See also *Lost & Found*)